GW00360176

Gemini

Dedication

For the memory of Gary Bailey, a new star in heaven.
For the memory of Frances Waxman, who always marched
to her own drum beat.

Acknowledgements
We gratefully acknowledge the help given to us by Lynn
Beddoe, Claire Champion, Anne Christie, Grant Griffiths
and Liz Dean who have all helped enormously with the
production of this book.

Gemini

Sasha Fenton and Jonathan Dee

P | **PARRAGON** |

This edition published 1996 for Parragon Books
Units 13–17 Avonbridge Industrial Estate
Atlantic Road
Avonmouth, Bristol BS11 9QD
by Diamond Books
77–85 Fulham Palace Road
Hammersmith, London W6 8JB

ISBN 0 75251 903 4

Phototypeset by Intype London Ltd
Printed in Great Britain

Contents

The Essential Gemini

Your **Ruling Planet** Your ruling body is Mercury. The Roman god Mercury was the swift-witted messenger of the gods, whose principal job was to do Jupiter's dirty work! He was the god of healing and magic, and also thieves.

Your **Symbol** Your symbol is the heavenly twins, Castor and Pollux. The symbol of the twins is known in many cultures, including that of the Native Americans. The Bible emphasises the rivalry of twins in the story of Cain and Abel.

Parts of the Body The upper respiratory system, the shoulders, arms, wrists and hands.

Your **Good Bits** Mental agility, adaptability, the ability to communicate and a sense of humour.

Your **Bad Bits** Lack of sympathy when others are ill or unhappy. Selfishness and self-absorption. Hopping from one idea to another. Telling lies when it suits you.

Your **Weaknesses** Chatting on the phone for hours. Smoking (a high proportion of Geminis smoke). Those who don't make a great fuss about cigarette smoke, which inevitably drifts across the room to them.

YOUR BEST DAY Wednesday, because it is associated with the Roman god Mercury, also your ruling planet.

YOUR WORST DAY Friday.

YOUR COLOURS Yellow, black-and-white check and multi-coloured mixtures.

CITIES London, Bruges, San Francisco, Melbourne.

COUNTRIES Wales, Japan, Indonesia.

HOLIDAYS You enjoy a good old-fashioned beach holiday where you can soak up the sun. You're happy anywhere that has a variety of shops, interesting places to eat out and plenty to see.

YOUR FAVOURITE CAR A small, fast sports car. Even if you have absolutely no money at all, you need to be mobile and, therefore, you will put up with any kind of broken-down transport rather than be without wheels.

YOUR FAVOURITE MEAL OUT Question: what does the Gemini make for dinner? Answer: reservations! You prefer simple foods like fish and chips or salads to over-cooked dishes or piles of unidentified mush. Geminis tend to enjoy Chinese food because it consists of tasty titbits, and many of you are vegetarians. Most of you are happy with a drink and a cigarette, plus the occasional tomato sandwich to keep you from keeling over.

YOUR FAVOURITE DRINK This is quite an addictive sign, and a great many Geminis drink a lot. Whether a light or a heavy drinker, most seem to enjoy spirits of all kinds, and either wine, beer or lager with a meal. Cocktails and mixed drinks are favourites too.

YOUR HERB Marjoram.

YOUR TREES Nut trees, especially the walnut.

YOUR FLOWERS Lily of the valley, lavender, orchid and the gladiolus.

YOUR ANIMALS Hyena, monkey, parrot, stork.

YOUR METAL Mercury.

YOUR GEMS There are various gems associated with your sign, including the agate, alexandrite and onyx.

MODE OF DRESS Anything stylish that allows you to move around quickly. High-fashion sports gear is ideal. You love clothes and will spend a lot of money on good items.

YOUR CAREERS Communication is the key for the Gemini at work: writer, journalist, teacher, telephonist, sales person, taxi-driver, courier, travel agent, flight attendant, pilot are all favoured occupations.

YOUR FRIENDS Your friends must be intelligent, humorous people who have interesting lives.

YOUR ENEMIES Dull, mean or crabby types. Quiet, introverted people or those who are spiteful and offensive.

YOUR FAVOURITE GIFT Stationery makes a good stocking-filler, while a good quality pen-and-pencil or maths set would also suit some of you. Airline tickets to a hot place would delight you, as would a hands-on day at a race track.

YOUR LUCKY NUMBER Your lucky number is 3. To find your lucky number on a raffle ticket or something similar, first add the number together. For example, if one of your lottery numbers is 28, add 2 + 8 to make 10; then add 1 + 0, to give the root number of 1. The number 316 on a raffle ticket works in the same way. Add 3 + 1 + 6 to make 10: then add 1 + 0, making 1. As your lucky number is any number that adds up to 3, numbers such as 21, 147 or 30 would do. A selection of lottery numbers should include at least some of the following: 3, 12, 30, 39 and 48.

Your Sun Sign

Gemini

Ruled by Mercury
21st May to 21st June

Gemini is a masculine, air sign and this makes you restless, adventurous, outgoing, curious and, sometimes, a nervous wreck.

You are easily bored and you thrive on variety. You need a job that is different from one day to the next, and you'll often try to get the more mundane tasks out of the way quickly. You have a reputation for knowing a little about a lot of things, but this is unfair and untrue; the chances are that you know a lot about at least one important subject, but you are interested in everything that's going on around you. You can chat on the 'phone and do six other things at the same time! Your curiosity also leads you to find out about a great many things, and you constantly try out new ideas on your friends and family. Geminis of both sexes like to live in neat and orderly surroundings, but you prefer not to do the housework yourself. If you are wise, you will choose a partner who is willing to take some of the cooking and cleaning off your hands. You enjoy being with young people, because you tend to stay young yourself throughout life. Some of you teach, or work with the young as a hobby.

You have a reputation for flirtatiousness but this is also somewhat unfounded. You love to chat to members of the opposite sex and you thoroughly enjoy parties and social occasions which allow you to mix with all kinds of people and ask them about their lives. Many of you are great travellers. Geminis make excellent journalists, due to a natural curiosity and an ability to write, talk and communicate ideas to others. Faithful in permanent relationships, you fear abandonment yourself and would, therefore, never want your partner to feel insecure. You remain close to your children and you take an intelligent interest in their lives, but you can try to interfere on occasions.

Some Geminis spend money like water, especially on clothes, eating out and travelling, but you tend to earn this money yourself rather than demand it from your partner. Most of you are generous, but you hate being taken for a fool or lending money which is not repaid. You need trust and freedom in a relationship and you respect a partner's need for independence. You may miss out on the joys of childhood, possibly because your parents were selfish or difficult, or for reasons beyond anyone's control. The chances are that you didn't get on well with your brothers and sisters or that you had a hard time at school. This leaves you with a need for a close and loving family of your own, and you may marry early in order to find this. If your marriage doesn't work out, you will eventually try to find someone else.

You are probably quite a clever business person, finding ingenious ways of making or saving money for yourself and the people you work for. You prefer to work near telephones, fax machines and among people because communication interests you. Many of you make excellent accountants. Having said that, you are clever with your hands and may be keen on repairing cars, making small items or knitting. Your nerves are your greatest enemy, and many of you are heavy smokers, relying on nicotine to calm you down when the going gets tough. Your sign does not, however, suggest that you are two-faced, or have a split personality – you just have many talents and friends to suit your many moods.

All the Other Sun Signs

Aries

21st March to 20th April

Ariens can get anything they want off the ground, but it may land back down again with a bump. Quick to think and to act, Ariens are often intelligent and have little patience with fools. This includes anyone who is slower than themselves.

They are not the tidiest of people and they are impatient with details, except when engaged upon their special subject; *then* Ariens can fiddle around for hours. They are willing to make huge financial sacrifices for their families and they can put up with relatives living with them as long as this leaves them free to do their own thing. Aries women are decisive and competitive at work but many are disinterested in homemaking. They might consider giving up a relationship if it interfered with their ambitions. Highly sexed and experimental, they are faithful while in love but, if love begins to fade, they start to look around. Ariens may tell themselves that they are only looking for amusement, but they may end up in a fulfilling relationship with someone else's partner. This kind of situation offers the continuity and emotional support which they need with no danger of boredom or entrapment.

Their faults are those of impatience and impetuosity, coupled with a hot temper. They can pick a furious row with a supposed adversary, tear him or her to pieces then walk away from the situation five minutes later, forgetting all about it. Unfortunately, the poor victim can't always shake off the effects of the row in quite the same way. However, Arien cheerfulness, spontaneous generosity and kindness make them the greatest friends to have.

Taurus

21st April to 21st May

These people are practical and persevering. Taureans are solid and reliable, regular in habits, sometimes a bit wet behind the ears and stubborn as mules. Their love of money and the comfort it can bring may make them very materialistic in outlook. They are most suited to a practical career which brings with it few surprises and plenty of money. However, they have a strong artistic streak which can be expressed in work, hobbies and interests.

Some Taureans are quick and clever, highly amusing and quite outrageous in appearance, but underneath this crazy exterior is a background of true talent and very hard work. This type may be a touch arrogant. Other Taureans hate to be rushed or hassled, preferring to work quietly and thoroughly at their own pace. They take relationships very seriously and make safe and reliable partners. They may keep their worries to themselves but they are not usually liars or sexually untrustworthy.

Being so very sensual as well as patient, these people make excellent lovers. Their biggest downfall comes later in life when they have a tendency to plonk themselves down in front of the television night after night, tuning out the rest of the world. Another problem with some

Taureans is their 'pet hate', which they'll harp on about at any given opportunity. Their virtues are common sense, loyalty, responsibility and a pleasant, non-hostile approach to others. Taureans are much brighter than anyone gives them credit, and it is hard to beat them in an argument because they usually know what they are talking about. If a Taurean is on your side, they make wonderful friends and comfortable and capable colleagues.

Cancer

22nd June to 23rd July

Cancerians look for security on the one hand and adventure and novelty on the other. They are popular because they really listen to what others are saying. Their own voices are attractive too. They are naturals for sales work and in any kind of advisory capacity. Where their own problems are concerned, they can disappear inside themselves and brood, which makes it hard for others to understand them. Cancerians spend a good deal of time worrying about their families and, even more so, about money. They appear soft but are very hard to influence.

Many Cancerians are small traders and many more work in teaching or the caring professions. They have a feel for history, perhaps collecting historical mementoes, and their memories are excellent. They need to have a home but they love to travel away from it, being happy in the knowledge that it is there waiting for them to come back to. There are a few Cancerians who seem to drift through life and expect other members of their family to keep them. Romantically, they prefer to be settled and they fear being alone. A marriage would need to be really bad before they consider leaving, and if they do, they soon look for a new partner. These people can be scoundrels in business because they hate parting with money once they have their hands on it. However, their charm and intelligence usually manage to get them out of trouble.

Leo

24th July to 23rd August

Leos can be marvellous company or a complete pain in the neck. Under normal circumstances, they are warm-hearted, generous, sociable and popular but they can be very moody and irritable when under pressure or under the weather. Leos put their heart and soul into whatever they are doing and they can work like demons for a while. However, they cannot keep up the pace for long and they need to get away, zonk out on the sofa and take frequent holidays. These people always appear confident and they look like true winners, but their confidence can suddenly evaporate, leaving them unsure and unhappy with their efforts. They are extremely sensitive to hurt and they cannot take ridicule or even very much teasing.

Leos are proud. They have very high standards in all that they do and most have great integrity and honesty, but there are some who are complete and utter crooks. These people can stand on their dignity and be very snobbish. Their arrogance can become insufferable and they can take their powers of leadership into the realms of bossiness. They are convinced that they should be in charge and they can be very obstinate. Some Leos love the status and lifestyle which proclaims their successes. Many work in glamour professions such as the airline and entertainment industries. Others spend their day communing with computers and other high-tech gadgetry. In loving relationships, they are loyal but only while the magic lasts. If boredom sets in, they often start looking around for fresh fields. They are the most generous and loving of people and they need to play affectionately. Leos are kind, charming and they live life to the full.

Virgo

24th August to 23rd September

Virgos are highly intelligent, interested in everything and everyone and happy to be busy with many jobs and hobbies. Many have some kind of specialised knowledge and most are good with their hands. Their nit-picking ways can infuriate their colleagues. They find it hard to discuss their innermost feelings and this can make them hard to understand. In many ways, they are happier doing something practical than dealing with relationships. These people can overdo the self-sacrificial bit and make themselves martyrs to other people's impractical lifestyles. They are willing to fit in with whatever is going on and they can adjust to most things, but they mustn't neglect their own needs.

Although excellent communicators and wonderfully witty conversationalists, Virgos prefer to express their deepest feelings by actions rather than words. Most avoid touching all but very close friends and family members and they find lovey-dovey behaviour embarrassing. These people can be very highly sexed and they may use this as a way of expressing love. Virgos are criticised a good deal as children and are often made to feel unwelcome in their childhood homes. They in turn become very critical of others and they can use this in order to wound.

Many Virgos overcome inhibitions by taking up acting, music, cookery or sports. Acting is particularly common to this sign because it allows them to put aside their fears and take on the mantle of someone quite different. They are shy and slow to make friends but when they do accept someone, they are the loyalest, gentlest and kindest of companions. They are great company and have a wonderful sense of humour.

Libra

24th September to 23rd October

Librans have a deceptive appearance, looking soft but being tough and quite selfish underneath. Astrological tradition tells us that this sign is dedicated to marriage, but a high proportion of them prefer to remain single, particularly when a difficult relationship comes to an end. These people are great to tell secrets to because they never listen to anything properly and promptly forget whatever is said. The confusion between their desire to co-operate with others and the need for self-expression is even more evident when at work. The best job is one where they are a part of an organisation but able to take responsibility and make their own decisions.

While some Librans are shy and lacking in confidence, others are strong and determined with definite leadership qualities. All need to find a job that entails dealing with others and which does not wear out their delicate nerves. All Librans are charming, sophisticated and diplomatic, but can be confusing for others. All have a strong sense of justice and fair play but most haven't the strength to take on a determinedly lame duck. They project an image which is attractive, chosen to represent their sense of status and refinement. Being inclined to experiment sexually, they are not the most faithful of partners and even goody-goody Librans are terrible flirts.

Scorpio

24th October to 22nd November

Reliable, resourceful and enduring, Scorpios seem to be the strong men and women of the zodiac. But are they really? They can be nasty at times, dishing out what they see as the truth, no matter how unwelcome. Their own feelings are sensitive and they are easily hurt, but they won't show any hurt or weakness in themselves to others. When they are very low or unhappy, this turns inwards, attacking their immune systems and making them ill. However, they have great resilience and they bounce back time and again from the most awful ailments.

Nobody needs to love and be loved more than a Scorpio, but their partners must stand up to them because they will give anyone they don't respect a very hard time indeed. They are the most loyal and honest of companions, both in personal relationships and at work. One reason for this is their hatred of change or uncertainty. Scorpios enjoy being the power behind the throne with someone else occupying the hot seat. This way, they can quietly manipulate everyone, set one against another and get exactly what they want from the situation.

Scorpios' voices are their best feature, often low, well-modulated and cultured and these wonderful voices are used to the full in pleasant persuasion. These people are neither as highly sexed nor as difficult as most astrology books make out, but they do have their passions (even if these are not always for sex itself) and they like to be thought of as sexy. They love to shock and to appear slightly dangerous, but they also make kind-hearted and loyal friends, superb hosts and gentle people who are often very fond of animals. Great people when they are not being cruel, stingy or devious!

Sagittarius

23rd November to 21st December

Sagittarians are great company because they are interested in everything and everyone. Broad-minded and lacking in prejudice, they are fascinated by even the strangest of people. With their optimism and humour, they are often the life and soul of the party, while they are in a good mood. They can become quite down-hearted, crabby and awkward on occasion, but not usually for long. They can be hurtful to others because they cannot resist speaking what they see as the truth, even if it causes embarrassment. However, their tactlessness is usually innocent and they have no desire to hurt.

Sagittarians need an unconventional lifestyle, preferably one which allows them to travel. They cannot be cooped up in a cramped environment and they need to meet new people and to explore a variety of ideas during their day's work. Money is not their god – they will work for a pittance if they feel inspired by the task. Their values are spiritual rather than material. Many are attracted to the spiritual side of life and may be interested in the Church, philosophy, astrology and other New Age subjects. Higher education and legal matters attract them because these subjects expand and explore intellectual boundaries. Long-lived relationships may not appeal because they need to feel free and unfettered, but they can do well with a self-sufficient and independent partner. Despite all this intellectualism and need for freedom, Sagittarians have a deep need to be cuddled and touched and they need to be supported emotionally.

Capricorn

22nd December to 20th January

Capricorns are patient, realistic and responsible and they take life seriously. They need security but they may find this difficult to achieve. Many live on a treadmill of work, simply to pay the bills and feed the kids. They will never shun family responsibilities, even caring for distant relatives if this becomes necessary. However, they can play the martyr while doing so. These people hate coarseness, they are easily embarrassed and they hate to annoy anyone. Capricorns believe fervently in keeping the peace in their families. This doesn't mean that they cannot stand up for themselves, indeed they know how to get their own way and they won't be bullied. They are adept at using charm to get around prickly people.

Capricorns are ambitious, hard working, patient and status-conscious and they will work their way steadily towards the top in any organisation. If they run their own businesses, they need a partner with more pizazz to deal with sales and marketing for them while they keep an eye on the books. Their nit-picking habits can infuriate others and some have a tendency to 'know best' and not to listen. These people work at their hobbies with the same kind of dedication that they put into everything else.

They are faithful and reliable in relationships and it takes a great deal to make them stray. If a relationship breaks up, they take a long time to get over it. They may marry very early or delay it until middle age when they are less shy. As an earth sign, Capricorns are highly sexed but they need to be in a relationship where they can relax and gain confidence. Their best attribute is their genuine kindness and their wonderfully dry, witty sense of humour.

Aquarius

21st January to 19th February

Clever, friendly, kind and humane, Aquarians are the easiest people to make friends with but probably the hardest to really know. They are often more comfortable with acquaintances than with those who are close to them. Being dutiful, they would never let a member of their family go without their basic requirements, but they can be strangely, even deliberately, blind to their underlying needs and real feelings. They are more comfortable with causes and their idealistic ideas than with the day-to-day routine of family life. Their homes may reflect this lack of interest by being rather messy, although there are other Aquarians who are almost clinically house proud.

Their opinions are formed early in life and are firmly fixed. Being patient with people, they make good teachers and are, themselves, always willing to learn something new. But are they willing to go out and earn a living? Some are, many are not. These people can be extremely eccentric in the way they dress or the way they live. They make a point of being 'different' and they can actually feel very unsettled and uneasy if made to conform, even outwardly. Their restless, sceptical minds mean that they need an alternative kind of lifestyle which stretches them mentally.

In relationships, they are surprisingly constant and faithful and they only stray when they know in their hearts that there is no longer anything useful to be gained from staying put.

Aquarians are often very attached to the first real commitment in their lives and they can even re-marry 5a previously divorced partner. Their sexuality fluctuates, perhaps peaking for some years then pushed aside while something else occupies their energies, then high again.

Many Aquarians are extremely highly sexed and very clever and active in bed.

Pisces

20th February to 20th March

This idealistic, dreamy, kind and impractical sign needs a lot of understanding. They have a fractured personality which has so many sides and so many moods that they probably don't even understand themselves. Nobody is more kind, thoughtful and caring, but they have a tendency to drift away from people and responsibilities. When the going gets rough, they get going! Being creative, clever and resourceful, these people can achieve a great deal and really reach the top, but few of them do. Some Pisceans have a self-destruct button which they press before reaching their goal. Others do achieve success and the motivating force behind this essentially spiritual and mystical sign is often money. Many Pisceans feel insecure, most suffer some experience of poverty at some time in their early lives and they grow into adulthood determined that they will never feel that kind of uncertainty again.

Pisceans are at home in any kind of creative or caring career. Many can be found in teaching, nursing and the arts. Some find life hard and are often unhappy; many have to make tremendous sacrifices on behalf of others. This may be a pattern which repeats itself from childhood, where the message is that the Piscean's needs always come last. These people can be stubborn, awkward, selfish and quite nasty when a friendship or relationship goes sour. This is because, despite their basically kind and gentle personality, there is a side which needs to be in charge of any relationship. Pisceans make extremely faithful partners as long as the romance doesn't evaporate and their partners treat them well. Problems occur if they are mistreated or rejected, if they become bored or restless or if their alcohol intake climbs over the danger level. The Piscean lover is a sexual fantasist, so in this sphere of life anything can happen!

You and Yours

What is it like to bring up a Gemini child? What kind of father does a Libran make? How does it feel to grow up with a Scorpio mother? Whatever your own sign is, how do you appear to your parents and how do you behave towards your children?

The Gemini Father

Gemini fathers are fairly laid back in their approach and, while they cope well with fatherhood, they can become bored with home life and try to escape from their duties. Some are so absorbed with work that they hardly see their offspring. At home, Gemini fathers will provide books, educational toys and as much computer equipment as the child can use, and they enjoy a family game of tennis.

The Gemini Mother

These mothers can be very pushy because they see education as the road to success. They encourage a child to pursue any interest and will sacrifice time and money for this. They usually have a job outside the home and may rely on other people to do some child minding for them. Their children cannot always count on coming home to a balanced meal, but they can talk to their mothers on any subject.

The Gemini Child

These children needs a lot of reassurance because they often feel like square pegs in round holes. They either do very well at school and incur the wrath of less able children, or they fail dismally and have to make it up later in life. They learn to read early and some have excellent mechanical ability, while others excel at sports. They get bored very easily and they can be extremely irritating.

The Aries Father

Arien men take the duties of fatherhood very seriously. They read to their children, take them on educational trips and expose them to art and music from an early age. They can push their children too hard or tyrannise the sensitive ones. The Aries father wants his children not only to *have* what he didn't have but also to *be* what he isn't. He respects those children who are high achievers and who can stand up to him.

The Aries Mother

Arien women love their children dearly and will make amazing sacrifices for them, but don't expect them to give up their jobs or their outside interests for motherhood. Competitive herself, this mother wants her children to be the best and she may push them too hard. However, she is kind hearted, affectionate and not likely to over-discipline them. She treats her offspring as adults and is well loved in return.

The Aries Child

Arien children are hard to ignore. Lively, noisy and demanding, they try to enjoy every moment of their childhood. Despite this, they lack confidence and need reassurance. Often clever but lacking in self-discipline, they need to be made to attend school each day and to do their homework. Active and competitive, these children excel in sports, dancing or learning to play a pop music instrument.

The Taurus Father

This man cares deeply for his children and wants the best for them, but he doesn't expect the impossible. He may lay the law down and he can be unsympathetic to the attitudes and interests of a new generation. He may frighten young children by shouting at them. Being a responsible parent, he offers a secure family base but he may find it hard to let them go when they want to leave.

The Taurus Mother

These women make good mothers due to their highly domesticated nature. Some are real earth mothers, baking bread and making wonderful toys and games for their children. Sane and sensible but not highly imaginative, they do best with a child who has ordinary needs and they get confused by those who are 'special' in any way. Taurean mothers are very loving but they use reasonable discipline when necessary.

The Taurus Child

Taurean children can be surprisingly demanding. Their loud voices and stubborn natures can be irritating. Plump, sturdy and strong, some are shy and retiring, while others can bully weaker children. Artistic, sensual and often musical, these children can lose themselves in creative or beautiful hobbies. They need to be encouraged to share and express love and also to avoid too many sweet foods.

The Cancer Father

A true family man who will happily embrace even step-children as if they were his own. Letting go of the family when they grow up is another matter. Cancerian sulks, moodiness and bouts of childishness can confuse or frighten some children, while his changeable attitude to money can make them unsure of what they should ask for. This father enjoys home making and child rearing and he may be happy to swap roles.

The Cancer Mother

Cancerian women are excellent home makers and cheerful and reasonable mothers, as long as they have a part-time job or an interest outside the house. They instinctively know when a child is unhappy and can deal with it in a manner which is both efficient and loving. These women have a reputation for clinging but most are quite realistic when the time comes for their brood to leave the nest.

The Cancer Child

These children are shy, cautious and slow to grow up. They may achieve little at school, 'disappearing' behind louder and more demanding classmates. They can be worriers who complain about every ache and pain or suffer from imaginary fears. They may take on the mother's role in the family, dictating to their sisters and brothers at times. Gentle and loving but moody and secretive, they need a lot of love and encouragement.

The Leo Father

These men can be wonderful fathers as long as they remember that children are not simply small and rather obstreperous adults. Leo fathers like to be involved with their children and encourage them to do well at school. They happily make sacrifices for their children and they truly want them to have the best, but they can be a bit too strict and they may demand too high a standard.

The Leo Mother

Leo mothers are very caring and responsible but they cannot be satisfied with a life of pure domesticity, and need to combine motherhood with a job. These mothers don't fuss about minor details. They're prepared to put up with a certain amount of noise and disruption, but they can be irritable and they may demand too much of their children.

The Leo Child

These children know almost from the day they are born that they are special. They are usually loved and wanted but they are also aware that a lot is expected from them. Leo children appear outgoing but they are surprisingly sensitive and easily hurt. They only seem to wake up to the need to study a day or so after they leave school, but they find a way to make a success of their lives.

The Virgo Father

These men may be embarrassed by open declarations of love and affection and find it hard to give cuddles and reassurance to small children. Yet they love their offspring dearly and will go to any lengths to see that they have the best possible education and outside activities. Virgoan men can become wrapped up in their work, forgetting to spend time relaxing and playing with their children.

The Virgo Mother

Virgoan women try hard to be good mothers because they probably had a poor childhood themselves. They love their children very much and want the best for them but they may be fussy about unnecessary details, such as dirt on the kitchen floor or the state of the children's school books. If they can keep their tensions and longings away from their children, they can be the most kindly and loving parents.

The Virgo Child

Virgoan children are practical and capable and can do very well at school, but they are not always happy. They don't always fit in and they may have difficulty making friends. They may be shy, modest and sensitive and they can find it hard to live up to their own impossibly high standards. Virgoan children don't need harsh discipline, they want approval and will usually respond perfectly well to reasoned argument.

The Libra Father

Libran men mean well, but they may not actually perform that well. They have no great desire to be fathers but welcome their children when they come along. They may slide out of the more irksome tasks by having an absorbing job or a series of equally absorbing hobbies which keep them occupied outside the home. These men do better with older children because they can talk to them.

The Libra Mother

Libran mothers are pleasant and easy-going but some of them are more interested in their looks, their furnishings and their friends than their children. Others are very loving and kind but a bit too soft, which results in their children not respecting them or walking all over them in later life. These mothers enjoy talking to their children and encouraging them to succeed.

The Libra Child

These children are charming and attractive and they have no difficulty in getting on with people. They make just enough effort to get through school and only do the household jobs they cannot dodge. They may drive their parents mad with their demands for the latest gadget or gimmick. However, their common sense, sense of humour and reasonable attitude to life makes harsh discipline unnecessary.

The Scorpio Father

These fathers can be really awful or absolutely wonderful, and there aren't any half-measures. Good Scorpio men provide love and security because they stick closely to their homes and families and are unlikely to do a disappearing act. Difficult ones can be loud and tyrannical. These proud men want their children to be the best.

The Scorpio Mother

These mothers are either wonderful or not really maternal at all, although they try to do their best. If they take to child rearing, they encourage their offspring educationally and in their hobbies. These mothers have no time for whiny or miserable children but they respect outgoing, talented and courageous ones and can cope with a handful.

The Scorpio Child

Scorpio children are very competitive, self-centred and unwilling to co-operate with brothers, sisters, teachers or anyone else when in an awkward mood. They can be deeply unreadable, living in a world of their own and filled with all kinds of strange angry feelings. At other times, they can be delightfully caring companions. They love animals, sports, children's organisations and group activities.

The Sagittarius Father

Sagittarian fathers will give their children all the education they can stand. They happily provide books, equipment and take their offspring out to see anything interesting. They may not always be available to their offspring, but they make up for it by surprising their families with tickets for sporting events or by bringing home a pet for the children. These men are cheerful and childlike themselves.

The Sagittarius Mother

This mother is kind, easy-going and pleasant. She may be very ordinary with suburban standards or she may be unbelievably eccentric, forcing the family to take up strange diets and filling the house with weird and wonderful people. Some opt out of child rearing by finding child minders while others take on other people's children and a host of animals in addition to their own.

The Sagittarius Child

Sagittarian children love animals and the outdoor life but they are just as interested in sitting around and watching the telly as the next child. These children have plenty of friends whom they rush out and visit at every opportunity. Happy and optimistic but highly independent, they cannot be pushed in any direction. Many leave home in late teens in order to travel.

The Capricorn Father

These are true family men who cope with housework and child rearing but they are sometimes too involved in work to spend much time at home. Dutiful and caring, these men are unlikely to run off with a bimbo or to leave their family wanting. However, they can be stuffy or out of touch with the younger generation. They encourage their children to do well and to behave properly.

The Capricorn Mother

Capricorn women make good mothers but they may be inclined to fuss. Being ambitious, they want their children to do well and they teach them to respect teachers, youth leaders and so on. These mothers usually find work outside the home in order to supplement the family income. They are very loving but they can be too keen on discipline and the careful management of pocket money.

The Capricorn Child

Capricorn children are little adults from the day they are born. They don't need much discipline or encouragement to do well at school. Modest and well behaved, they are almost too good to be true. However, they suffer badly with their nerves and can be prone to ailments such as asthma. They need to be taught to let go, have fun and enjoy their childhood. Some are too selfish or ambitious to make friends with other children.

The Aquarian Father

Some Aquarian men have no great desire to be fathers but they make a reasonable job of it when they have to. They cope best when their children are reasonable and intelligent but, if they are not, they tune out and ignore them. Some Aquarians will spend hours inventing games and toys for their children while all of them value education and try to push their children.

The Aquarian Mother

Some of these mothers are too busy putting the world to rights to see what is going on in their own family. However, they are kind, reasonable and keen on education. They may be busy outside the house but they often take their children along with them. They are not fussy homemakers, and are happy to have all the neighbourhood kids in the house. They respect a child's dignity.

The Aquarian Child

These children may be demanding when very young but they become much more reasonable when at school. They are easily bored and need outside interests. They have many friends and may spend more time in other people's homes than in their own. Very stubborn and determined, they make it quite clear from an early age that they intend to do things their own way. These children are likely to suffer from nerves.

The Pisces Father

Piscean men fall into one of two categories. Some are kind and gentle, happy to take their children on outings and to introduce them to art, culture, music or sport. Others are disorganised and unpredictable. The kindly fathers don't always push their children. They encourage their kids to have friends and a pet or two.

The Pisces Mother

Piscean mothers may be lax and absent-minded but they love their children and are usually loved in return. Many are too disorganised to run a perfect household so meals, laundry etc. can be hit and miss, but their children prosper despite this, although many learn to reverse the mother and child roles. These mothers teach their offspring to appreciate animals and the environment.

The Pisces Child

These sensitive children may find life difficult and they can get lost among stronger, more demanding brothers and sisters. They may drive their parents batty with their dreamy attitude and they can make a fuss over nothing. They need a secure and loving home with parents who shield them from harsh reality while encouraging them to develop their imaginative and psychic abilities.

Your Rising Sign

What is a Rising Sign?

Your rising sign is the sign of the zodiac which was climbing up over the eastern horizon the moment you were born. This is not the same as your Sun sign; your Sun sign depends upon your date of birth, but your rising sign depends upon the time of day that you were born, combined with your date and place of birth.

The rising sign modifies your Sun sign character quite considerably, so when you have worked out which is your rising sign, read page 36 to see how it modifies your Sun sign. Then take a deeper look by going back to 'All the Other Sun Signs' on page 7 and read the relevant Sun sign material there to discover more about your ascendant (rising sign) nature.

Can Your Rising Sign Tell You More About Your Future?

When it comes to tracking events, the rising sign is equal in importance to the Sun sign. So, if you want a more accurate forecast when reading newspapers or magazines, you should read the horoscope for your rising sign as well as your Sun sign. In the case of books such as this, you should really treat yourself to two – one to correspond with your rising sign, and another for your usual Sun sign, and read both each day!

One final point is that the sign that is opposite your rising sign (or ascendant) is known as your *descendant*. This shows what you want from other people, and it may give a clue as to your choice of friends, colleagues and lovers (see the chart on page 35). So once you have found your rising sign and read the character interpretation, check out the character reading for your descendant to see what you are looking for in others.

Using the Rising Sign Finder

Please bear in mind that this method is approximate – if you want to be really sure of your rising sign, you should contact an astrologer. However, this system will work with reasonable accuracy wherever you were born, although it is worth checking the Sun and ascendant combination in the following pages and reading the Sun sign character on pages 7–18 for the signs both before and after the rising sign you think is yours. For example, if you think that Capricorn is your rising sign, read the Gemini/Sagittarius, Gemini/Capricorn and Gemini/Aquarius combinations. Then check out the Sun sign character readings for Sagittarius, Capricorn and Aquarius on pages 14, 15 and 16. You will soon see which rising sign fits your personality best.

How to Begin

Read through this section while following the example on page 34. Even if you only have a vague idea of your birth time, you won't find this method difficult; just go for a rough time of birth and then read the Sun sign information for that sign to see if it fits your personality. If you seem to be more like the sign that comes before or after it, then it is likely that you were born a little earlier or later than your assumed time of birth. Don't forget to deduct an hour for summertime births.

1. Look at the illustration below. You will notice that it has the time of day arranged around the outer circle. It looks a bit like a clock face, but it is different because it shows the whole 24–hour day in two-hour blocks.

2. Write the astrological symbol that represents the Sun (a circle with a dot in the middle) in the segment that corresponds to your time of birth. (If you were born during Daylight Saving or British Summer Time, deduct one hour from your birth time.) Our example shows someone who was born between 2 a.m. and 4 a.m.

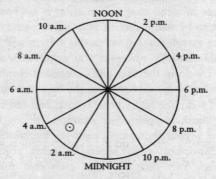

3. Now write the name of your sign or the symbol for your sign on the line which is at the end of the block of time that your Sun falls into. Our example shows a person who was born between 2 a.m. and 4 a.m. under the sign of Pisces.

4. Either write in the names of the zodiac signs or use the symbols in their correct order (see the key opposite) around the chart in an anti-clockwise direction.

KEY:

♈ Aries   ♋ Cancer   ♎ Libra   ♑ Capricorn

♉ Taurus   ♌ Leo   ♏ Scorpio   ♒ Aquarius

♊ Gemini   ♍ Virgo   ♐ Sagittarius   ♓ Pisces

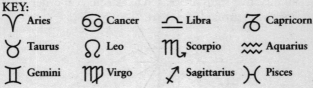

5. The sign that appears on the left-hand side is your rising sign, or ascendant. The example shows a person born with the Sun in Pisces and with Aquarius rising. Incidentally, the example chart also shows Leo in the descendant.

Here is another example for you to run through, just to make sure that you have grasped the idea correctly. This example is for a more awkward time of birth, being exactly on the line between two different blocks of time. This example is for a person with a Capricorn Sun sign who was born at 10 a.m.

1. The Sun is placed exactly on the 10 a.m. line.
2. The sign of Capricorn is placed on the 10 a.m. line.

3. All the other signs are placed in astrological order (anti-clockwise) around the chart.

4. This person has the Sun in Capricorn and Pisces rising, and therefore with Virgo on the descendant.

How Your Rising Sign Modifies Your Sun Sign
Gemini with Aries Rising

You could have a very outgoing personality with the ability to inspire others, but you may not be too gentle with their feelings.

Gemini with Taurus Rising

You could have a real head for figures, choosing to work as an accountant or a banker. You are keen on art, music and craft work.

Gemini with Gemini Rising

Your childhood difficulties take a long time to shake off and you may have to wait until middle age to reach your potential. If you were born before dawn you will be more confident than if you were born after dawn.

Gemini with Cancer Rising

You are more quiet and gentle than the average Gemini. You are probably drawn to work in one of the caring professions, but you like money too.

Gemini with Leo Rising

You need a good standard of living and you probably work hard to create this. You get on well with all kinds of people and you are particularly fond of young people.

Gemini with Virgo Rising

You are an excellent communicator with a talent for languages, teaching or writing. You can drive yourself nuts worrying about nothing.

Gemini with Libra Rising

You are great company and you are always bang up-to-date in your thinking. You could make a success of a career in the legal profession or as an international business person.

Gemini with Scorpio Rising

You are far more intense than the average Gemini and you can feel passionate about your beliefs. Your childhood could have left you with a fear of abandonment or of financial insecurity.

Gemini with Sagittarius Rising

You seek to protect your personal freedom and you may find it hard to settle down into a conventional lifestyle. You are very excited by ideas and travel.

Gemini with Capricorn Rising

You are one of the world's hardest workers, being ambitious for yourself and your family. You may have suffered poverty or deprivation in childhood.

Gemini with Aquarius Rising

You are excited by ideas and you may choose a lifestyle that allows you to explore them. Communications could play a large part in your career.

Gemini with Pisces Rising

You are more quiet and home-loving than the average Gemini, and you could also be drawn to mystical or psychic matters. You may choose to work from home.

Gemini in Love

You need:

RELIABILITY You have had enough unreliable people in your life to appreciate a sane and stable partner. Your lover should be calm and unflappable and able to cope with your nerves and depression.

SAFETY Gemini women can attract agressive partners, so you must make sure that you recognise any sign of this before you get trapped. Men need a woman who is a little motherly and who gives you a sense of security.

VARIETY You are easily bored, so a partner who has a very regular routine to his life and no imagination wouldn't suit you at all. You need someone who will spring little surprises on you and take you out regularly.

You give:

REASSURANCE what it is to feel insecure and unprotected, so you do your best to make a partner feel that life is under control and that you can cope. You may be moody but you are always there.

VARIETY You won't bore your partner by always being the same, you like to vary everything from meals to lifestyle to lovemaking. You are always ready for an outing or to meet interesting people.

ENCOURAGEMENT You stand by and encourage a lover in all their schemes, even when things don't work out entirely as expected. You may worry, but you don't undermine a partner's confidence.

What You Can Expect From the Other Zodiac Signs

ARIES *Truth, honesty, playfulness.* You can expect an open and honest relationship with no hidden agendas. Your Arien lover will be a bit childish at times, however.

TAURUS *Security, stability, comfort.* The Taurean will stand by you and try to improve your financial position. They will create a beautiful home and garden for you.

CANCER *Emotional security, companionship, help.* Cancerians will never leave you stranded at a party or alone when suffering from the flu. They always lend a hand when asked.

LEO *Affection, fun, loyalty.* Leo lovers are very steadfast and they would avenge anyone who hurt one of their family. They enjoy romping and playing affectionate love games.

VIRGO *Clear thinking, kindness, humour.* Virgoans make intelligent and amusing partners. They can be critical but are never unkind. They take their responsibility towards you seriously.

LIBRA *Fair-play, sensuality, advice.* Librans will listen to your problems and give balanced and sensible advice. They are wonderfully inventive, and are affectionate lovers too.

SCORPIO *Truth, passion, loyalty.* Scorpios will take your interests as seriously as they do their own. They will stick by you when the going gets tough and they won't flannel you.

SAGITTARIUS *Honesty, fun, novelty.* Theses lovers will never bore you and they'll keep up with whatever pace you set. They seek the truth and they don't keep their feelings hidden.

CAPRICORN *Companionship, common sense, laughter.* Capricorns enjoy doing things together and they won't leave you in the lurch when the going gets tough. They can make you laugh too.

AQUARIUS *Stimulation, friendship, sexuality.* Aquarians are friends as well as lovers. They are great fun because you never know what they are going to do next, in or out of bed.

PISCES *Sympathy, support, love.* These romantic lovers never let you down. They can take you with them into their personal fantasy world and they are always ready for a laugh.

Which Sign Are You Compatible With?

Gemini/Aries
Good combination, unless the Arien is too bossy or selfish.

Gemini/Taurus
You either complement each other well or can't stand each other.

Gemini/Gemini
Either mutual understanding or both demanding attention at once.

Gemini/Cancer
Cancer will mother Gemini and Gemini will love it.

Gemini/Leo
Gemini provides inspiration for Leo, and Leo protects Gemini.

Gemini/Virgo
Many shared interests but both may lack common sense.

Gemini/Libra
Either excellent combination or both looking for too much.
Gemini/Scorpio
Scorpio will dominate Gemini, both will use sarcasm
Gemini/Sagittarius
Sagittarius makes Gemini laugh and they share intellectual interests.
Gemini/Capricorn
Not a bad combination, especially for business.
Gemini/Aquarius
Excellent combination as long as Aquarius is not too detached.
Gemini/Pisces
Pisces can irritate Gemini but this can work nevertheless.

Gemini in 1997

Your Year Ahead

Love

You will start the year making some kind of major change in your relationship situation. Some of you will decide that you are getting nowhere with your current lover and that you need your freedom. Others will decide to settle into a real life-long commitment. Your attitude to love and what you want from a relationship is changing and from this point onwards, you will be seeking a more intellectual rapport from lovers. Some of you may be building a home or putting a joint business idea together and this looks quite well starred for you.

Some of you may fall for someone who is very different to you, or you may be drawn to a foreigner or to someone whom you meet while travelling. Joint financial matters will be far less uncertain and money will no longer be a bar to your chances of happiness. An older friend could become an important factor in your life this year.

Money

If your money matters are tied up with the fortunes of a lover or a business partnership, this will work to your advantage early in the year. Partnership matters that involve finances are all looking good now. You may have some kind of legal situation to handle and this too will bring money your way. Your best chances for earning money will come during the early summer, but you will need to keep a tight control on all financial matters during the autumn. This particularly applies to householders, or to those who are moving house at this time. You can afford to take a few chances with money this year.

Luck

The late summer and early autumn months will not be particularly lucky for you, so avoid speculating at this time. However, the spring and early summer look very good indeed for all gambles and speculative ventures. If you are house-hunting, you could find your dream home this spring, and any legal or official matters will go well then. Travel is particularly well starred in February and again in the late summer. Those of you who are looking for romance could find it while on, near or over the high seas in late August. An irritating situation will come to an end in September, clearing the way for new enterprises.

Signs and Symbols

The table at the beginning of each month shows your general trends for the month ahead. The symbols are very easy to understand because the hearts show the state of your love life, the stars tell you how your work is likely to go, the dollar signs tell you whether this will be a good month for money, the heartbeat graphs show your general health and energy levels and the horse shoes tell you whether this will be a lucky month or not.

The Aspects and their Astrological Meanings

CONJUNCT This shows important events which are usually, but not always, good.

SEXTILE Good, particularly for work and mental activity.

SQUARE Difficult, challenging.

TRINE Great for romance, family life and creativity.

OPPOSITE Awkward, depressing, challenging.

INTO This shows when a particular planet enters a new sign of the zodiac, thus setting off a new phase or a new set of circumstances.

DIRECT When a planet resumes normal direct motion.

RETROGRADE When a planet begins to apparently go backwards.

VOID When the Moon makes no aspect to any planet.

January at a Glance

LOVE	♥	♥	♥		
WORK	★	★	★	★	★
MONEY	$				
FITNESS	⊕				
LUCK	∪				

Wednesday, 1st January
Moon sextile Pluto

Happy New Year! If you are interested in love, sex and romance, then this is your day! You could find yourself tremendously attracted to a fascinating member of the opposite sex or, alternatively, you could find someone fancying you. If you are already firmly settled in a committed relationship, then this is the day to inject a little extra romance.

Thursday, 2nd January
Sun conjunct Mercury

Approach contracts and agreements with caution today. That's not to say that they are bad things to get involved with, just that you've got to play your cards close to your chest to make the most of them. You have the ability to handle any negotiations with ease since your shrewdness gives you the edge over any opponents. You'll have no trouble with small print.

Friday, 3rd January
Mars into Libra

Mars moves into a very creative area of your chart now, so if there is a project that you would like to get started upon, Mars will give you the drive and energy with which to do it. This is a good day for any kind of sporting or energetic pursuit, so if you want to practice your skills or get ready for some kind of future competition, then get down to it today.

Saturday, 4th January
Moon sextile Sun

If you need to find the right person to do a particular job for you, you should be able to do this with ease. Your mood is good now and you have the happy inner feeling that you are on the right track in many areas of your life.

Sunday, 5th January
Moon sextile Jupiter

The lunar aspect to Jupiter shows that this is a lucky day. If you've had any nagging ailments, your symptoms should ease as your general state of health improves. Stress levels should be reduced as your work worries are lessened.

Monday, 6th January
Mars opposite Saturn

One can't expect an easy day when Mars opposes Saturn, and when this unfortunate combination occurs in areas associated with leisure and friendships, one can't really expect these to go smoothly either. Frayed tempers and irritable people will be far too common today.

Tuesday, 7th January
Moon conjunct Venus

If you are a man or if you are reading this on behalf of a

man, you can expect something very romantic and pleasant to happen. If you happen to be a woman, then you can expect to have some kind of pleasant social event in the company of other women today. All working relationships, partnerships, marriages or other friendships will be at their best today.

Wednesday, 8th January
Moon conjunct Mercury

A declaration of love is certain today as the Moon conjuncts Mercury in your house of passion. This could be the start of something truly spectacular in your love life, and you'll be able to talk freely about the most intimate needs and desires now. There's no room for embarrassment when there's such a harmony between two people.

Thursday, 9th January
Jupiter conjunct Neptune

Follow your instincts in all money matters today. It doesn't matter what advice you receive, your intuition will unerringly guide you through the most complex financial dealings.

Friday, 10th January
Venus into Capricorn

Venus enters the area of your chart that is closely involved with love and sex today. Oddly enough, this aspect can bring the end of a difficult relationship, or just as easily begin a great new romance. If you have been dating but haven't yet got around to 'mating', this could be the start of something wonderful. Your emotional life over the next two or three weeks should be something to remember, that's for sure!

Saturday, 11th January
Venus square Saturn

You may find yourself fighting a losing battle over someone else's extravagance or stupidity. You could be the one who has to pay for someone else's mistakes and the situation could even rub off on you, so much so that your good name is dragged through the mud. This may not be quite as bad as it sounds, but you will certainly find it hard to get others to see sense or to co-operate with you today.

Sunday, 12th January
Mercury direct

Mercury resumes its direct motion from today, so a lot of the confusions that have plagued joint finances and investments will now end. Your mind is clearer on these matters than it has been in ages so cast your eye over all budgetary affairs just to make sure that all is well.

Monday, 13th January
Moon sextile Sun

Your inner feelings are very much in harmony with everything that is going on around you today. You feel that your bosses and colleagues are on the right track and that you are doing exactly the right thing for your career.

Tuesday, 14th January
Moon square Venus

If you fancy an undemanding day with plenty of peace and harmony, we're afraid you're due for a rude awakening. No one has the slightest intention of leaving you to your own devices now. Well-meaning friends will urge you to be social and to get out and enjoy yourself, but all they manage to do is make you irritable. If you really do crave solitude you'll have to unplug the 'phone, ignore the door bell and pretend to be out.

Wednesday, 15th January
Mercury square Mars

Watch what you say and what you do today. Your mood is irritable and some may, unwisely, take you for granted or expect your good nature to stretch just that little bit too far. . . . with explosive results!

Thursday, 16th January
Moon square Uranus

This is a troublesome day, professionally speaking. The harsh aspect between the Moon and the disruptive planet Uranus sets off a minor tremor through your entire working world. It may be that a boardroom coup affects everyone lower down the ladder. Whatever the cause of the uncertainty, it's best to keep your head down and get on with your own job. Don't give in to the temptation to gossip, because this will only make the rumour mill spin faster.

Friday, 17th January
Sun conjunct Neptune

You are in an escapist mood today, and you may not be the only one! It seems that your partner is also feeling like getting away from it all. You may be strongly drawn to water now, so take a visit to any local beauty spot by the sea, or close to a river or lake. You and your lover will find this spiritually refreshing.

Saturday, 18th January
Moon sextile Saturn

You are on the right track, and other people will soon confirm this for you. Older people could be quite helpful to you now, either in connection with some kind of official matter or to do with something of a social nature.

Sunday, 19th January
Sun conjunct Jupiter

You or your lover could have a real stroke of luck today, but it is equally possible that you will both be able to see some kind of opportunity for advancement now. You are in one of those phases where it is difficult for you to initiate action or to take charge of events but, even though it is other people who seem to be ruling your existence now, you will be happy with the outcome.

Monday, 20th January
Sun into Aquarius

The Sun moves into your solar ninth house today to stay for one month. This is a good time to travel overseas, explore new neighbourhoods or take up an interest in spiritual matters. You may find yourself keen to read about religious or philosophical subjects or even to discover the world of psychic healing.

Tuesday, 21st January
Jupiter into Aquarius

Jupiter moves into its own natural home today, giving you a yearning for adventure beyond the present narrow confines of your life. For many, this will mean travel to far-off exotic places to experience cultures, thoughts and attitudes that are different from your own.

Wednesday, 22nd January
Mars sextile Pluto

When you know something is absolutely right, you'll move heaven and earth to get to it today. No amount of cautious persuasion will dissuade you from a romantic course that others will see as totally impulsive. Follow your heart because it will lead you in the right direction.

Thursday, 23rd January
Full Moon

This is likely to be a really awkward day for any kind of travelling that you have to do. A vehicle could let you down just when you most need it, or the public transport that you usually rely upon could suddenly disappear from the face of the earth.

Friday, 24th January
Sun conjunct Uranus

The solar conjunction with Uranus gives an injection of vitality to your relationship today. Try not to have preconceptions because you are about to be amazed by a partner's suggestions or actions now. Be open to new ideas, and don't feel threatened by developments in the life of someone close. The unattached may find a prospective mate in an unusual place or at an odd time.

Saturday, 25th January
Sun trine Mars

This is a good day for travelling and also for sporting activities. The combination of the Sun and Mars gives you the urge to be on the move, so anything that keeps you too long in any one pace will be resented.

Sunday, 26th January
Mars trine Uranus

You are going through a strange phase when unusual things seem to be happening to you and today is no exception. You may be filled with artistic inspiration and even a touch of real creative genius. Alternatively, you may find an ingenious way of solving a mechanical problem of some kind. Love-making will be intense and this could be the making of a troubled relationship.

Monday, 27th January
Moon trine Venus

A truly romantic interlude could turn into real passion today. You seem to have the kind of magnetic charisma that's guaranteed to make you irresistible to the opposite sex. Even if all you end up doing is sitting about at home with your loved one, make this as sexy and loving an occasion as you can. Set the scene with perfume, dim the lights and play some soft music tonight!

Tuesday, 28th January
Moon trine Jupiter

A convivial atmosphere takes hold as the Moon contacts Jupiter, spreading a little happiness around you. Negative moods are now forgiven and forgotten as harmonious influences lift your spirits. Try to make a special effort to show the more romantic side of your nature and take some time out for an intimate celebration to remember.

Wednesday, 29th January
Moon square Mercury

Any agreements concerning such sensitive issues as inheritance, investments or even alimony will go nowhere if you give in to an emotional outburst today. Feelings are running high, so it's more important than ever that you keep a cool head. Don't let your heart intrude into matters of finance.

Thursday, 30th January
Moon square Neptune

The cost of fun exceeds inflation today. What you want to do is likely to be expensive, just at a time when bills or other pressing financial demands land on your doorstep. I doubt if you'll worry about cost now . . . but there's always tomorrow!

Friday, 31st January
Moon square Uranus

This is going to be a difficult day for family issues. You will have one opinion that you'll stick to through thick and thin, but your partner is likely to be equally as dogged in opposition. Eventually you will have to compromise, but I doubt that either of you will be prepared to give an inch today. The only peace to be found now is outside your home.

February at a Glance

LOVE	♥	♥	♥		
WORK	★	★	★	★	
MONEY	$	$			
FITNESS	〽	〽			
LUCK	∪	∪	∪	∪	

Saturday, 1st February
Venus conjunct Neptune

You seem to be on a better wavelength with those around you. It seems that they have been harbouring dreams, ideas and plans for the future that may conflict with your own. However, if you sit down and talk things over now you may be able to reach a compromise that makes everyone happy. Your partner is in a particularly romantic frame of mind, so relax and enjoy it.

Sunday, 2nd February
Moon conjunct Pluto

Relationship matters are vitally important to you, and you must try to get any problems out into the open and solved now that you have an opportunity to do so. You may think that your lover is trying to manipulate you, and you could be right, but as long as you are aware of his or her machinations there's a chance to stop them and let the light of truth shine through. Despite all this, you share a lot of love.

Monday, 3rd February
Venus into Aquarius

Venus enters your solar ninth house of exploration this month, and this may make you slightly restless. Venus is concerned with the pleasures of life and also with leisure activities of all kinds, so explore such ideas as your sporting interests, or, perhaps listening to interesting music or going to art galleries and the like. You may want to travel somewhere new and interesting soon.

Tuesday, 4th February
Moon square Saturn

You may come up against sticky situations of an official or governmental kind. Something really irritating such as a parking fine is a distinct possibility! You could be invited to serve on a jury or to arbitrate in some other unpleasant manner in connection with something that has nothing to do with you personally.

Wednesday, 5th February
Uranus sextile Pluto

If you and your partner decide to take a spur-of-the-moment holiday today, this will work well for you. It's a good idea to plan a trip today or to get away for any kind of short break. If you are alone, you may meet someone new and interesting as a result of travelling. Your sex appeal seems to be high just now, so you'll have no difficulty in attracting a member of the opposite sex today!

Thursday, 6th February
Mars retrograde

Mars turns to retrograde motion today, suggesting that life will slow down somewhat over the next few weeks. Mars happens to be in your own sign just now, so you will notice its effects quite strongly. Women who are reading this may find it hard to get your man to behave in quite the way that you would like. Some of you may complain that your lover is home too much and under your feet, while others will complain of a lover's absence.

Friday, 7th February
New Moon

The New Moon in your house of adventure urges you to push ahead with new projects. You're in a self-confident mood, and feel able to tackle anything the world throws at you. There's a lure of the exotic today as well, as far-off places exert a powerful attraction. Think again about widening your personal horizons, by travel or in taking up an educational course. Intellectually you're on top form and your curiosity is boundless.

Saturday, 8th February
Mercury conjunct Neptune

You could hear something to your advantage today. The

news may come from an unexpected source, but it will be good to hear, whatever it is. You may have some kind of unusual psychic experience today or you could have a particularly startling and memorable dream. Dreams can come true, you know.

Sunday, 9th February
Jupiter sextile Saturn

This rare combination of Jupiter and Saturn turns your mind to serious concerns today. You may feel the need to improve your qualifications or undertake a course of study in a subject that fascinates you. Travel is also on the cards under the influence of these giant planets.

Monday, 10th February
Moon conjunct Saturn

Although you usually have no patience with petty rules and mind-numbing red tape, today you can handle the most complex document with ease. Half the battle is won when you know your rights, so don't be put off by irritating officials or long-winded forms because they'll be no match for your ingenuity and persistence. Legal affairs can be safely dealt with now because you have a superb eye for detail, not to mention a homing instinct for a loophole!

Tuesday, 11th February
Mercury conjunct Jupiter

This is be a wonderful day to start some kind of partnership or joint enterprise. The chance of success in any kind of business or money-making venture is very good, although even personal or loving partnerships could get off on a good footing. The problem is that any loving partnership that is started now could be based on practical matters or a financial arrangement rather than love.

Wednesday, 12th February
Moon square Neptune

Gullibility is the problem today. The lunar aspect to Neptune makes you rather susceptible to sob stories, glib liars and con merchants. Take care when even close friends spin you a tale. It wouldn't be wise to part with any cash at all at the moment.

Thursday, 13th February
Mercury conjunct Uranus

It's an important day to talk thorough any radical plans and schemes with your partner. If you keep everything to yourself, you'll be thought to be eccentric at best, downright weird at worst. You may be open to new and exciting ideas, but your partner may be of a more conservative frame of mind. Take time to explain your actions and intentions.

Friday, 14th February
Jupiter sextile Pluto

Your affections could be pretty fickle even on St Valentine's day, since one person could not possibly hold your attention for long. Perhaps you will discover someone who is not as susceptible to your charms as you would like, and you could set out on a campaign of amorous pursuit.

Saturday, 15th February
Mars opposite Saturn

You fancy having some fun, but many of your friends are too caught up in their own worries to be good companions. This could be a rather frustrating day since no one else seems willing to join you in frivolous distractions.

Sunday, 16th February
Jupiter conjunct Uranus

Anything could happen today! Jupiter meets up with the eccentric Uranus and this could send you off on a journey of discovery. Don't plan anything because under the influence of these planets, you could be off on the next plane to who knows where!

Monday, 17th February
Moon square Mars

Any spare cash will burn a hole in your pocket this Monday because you'll be set on a spending spree of outrageous extravagance. It's not the necessities you need worry about, but the more useless an item, the more you'll want it. In some ways this is actually a reaction to too much thrift in your life, but try to hold back when your purchasing power isn't up to a spending spree.

Tuesday, 18th February
Sun into Pisces

The Sun moves decisively into your horoscopic area of ambition from today, bringing in a spell when your worldly progress will achieve absolute priority. You need to feel that what you are doing is worthwhile and has more meaning than simply paying the bills. You may feel the urge to change you career, to make a long-term commitment to a worthwhile cause, or simply to demand recognition for past efforts. However this ambitious phase manifests itself, you can be sure that your prospects are considerably boosted from now on.

Wednesday, 19th February
Saturn trine Pluto

The rare aspect of Saturn and Pluto can't be pinned down to one day. It is a major influence that has been affecting your personal relationships and your dealings with friends for some time. At least transformations that occur will be beneficial to all concerned.

Thursday, 20th February
Moon opposite Jupiter

It's a very restless day as the Moon opposes Jupiter. You're likely to feel bored and stifled by the familiar and you yearn for a little adventure. Travel may be fraught with delays, so it may be wisest to confine yourself to expanding your knowledge via reading rather than risking a lengthy traffic jam.

Friday, 21st February
Moon opposite Venus

You seem to be giving up the thought of becoming a hard-headed business person today and becoming a dreamy, sensitive and kindly soul instead. Your soft centre is showing through your usual crusty exterior and your response to others will be tender and affectionate. This is a marvellous day on which to whisper sweet nothings to your lover, and also to steer clear of any serious negotiating.

Saturday, 22nd February
Full Moon

The Full Moon today focuses firmly on family and domestic issues. Perhaps it's time for some straight talking, because this is the best opportunity you'll get to put an end to home-based or emotional problems. In some ways it's time to put your cards on the table, but you should also take some share of the blame in family affairs. Apart from such personal concerns it's time to speak to someone in authority about your ambitions.

Sunday, 23rd February
Sun square Pluto

Your husband, wife, lover or business partner may be in a particularly crafty and manipulative mood at the moment. You have a clear idea of what you want out of life, but their ideas may be different. It would be better if your other half simply told you what they wanted and tried to reach a compromise. Unfortunately they don't seem to want to go about this in a straightforward manner, choosing to try to persuade you that what they want is also in your best interests.

Monday, 24th February
Moon conjunct Mars

Your entire chart is energised by the Moon's conjunction with Mars today. This should inspire and activate all the romantic potentials in your life. The trouble is that you could get a little big-headed now, so you'll have to guard against being just a shade too forceful, especially with a lover. Don't be too impulsive and domineering and you won't spoil a splendid day.

Tuesday, 25th February
Moon opposite Saturn

You may find yourself out of sympathy with other members of the family who belong to different generations. It may be your parents or your in-laws who get you down today or it may be the children who are being impossible. There is very little opportunity for escape and freedom seems far away. Grin and bear it for the time being.

Wednesday, 26th February
Moon square Neptune

This isn't the best day to concentrate on anything too important. Your judgement is likely to be flawed and it would be too easy to make some serious financial mistakes. The trouble is that your emotions are colouring your judgement, and it will be difficult to think logically.

Thursday, 27th February
Venus into Pisces

Venus moves into your solar house of ambition and prominence from today. If you're involved in any career in the arts, beautification, entertainment or public relations then you're bound to do well over the next few weeks. Those who work for women bosses won't do badly either since a female influence in the workplace will aid your ambitions. Since Venus is the planet of charisma, use diplomacy to solve professional problems. You can hardly fail to win with such a capacity for charm.

Friday, 28th February
Mercury into Pisces

There's a certain flexibility entering your career structure as indicated by the presence of Mercury in your solar area of ambition. You can now turn your acute mind to all sorts of career problems and solve them to everyone's satisfaction, and your own advantage. Your powers of persuasion will be heightened from now on, ensuring that you get your own way. Those seeking work should attend interviews because your personality will shine.

March at a Glance

LOVE	♥				
WORK	★	★			
MONEY	$	$			
FITNESS	🅦	🅦	🅦		
LUCK	☡				

Saturday, 1st March
Saturn sextile Uranus

The major aspect between Saturn and Uranus has been in effect for some months now and will continue to be a feature for some time to come. Travel, educational affairs and international connections are all stimulated under this beneficial influence.

Sunday, 2nd March
Moon square Sun

Some peace and quiet is the order of the day . . . if, that is, you can find some. There are still a lot of demands made upon you but you need some time to yourself, perhaps engaged in a favourite hobby to refresh your spirit. Too much interference from others will only result in you losing your temper. Put up a 'Do Not Disturb' sign; you'll feel better for a little solitude.

Monday, 3rd March
Venus square Pluto

Watch out for sexual harassment at your place of work today. If someone says or does something objectionable, then tell them so. Don't let them get away with this, because they will only think that they have licence to continue with their unkind behaviour. Guard against being manipulated by others now. Keep a clear eye on your own goals and don't allow others to distract you.

Tuesday, 4th March
Mercury conjunct Venus

Don't hide your light under a bushel today! Set out to impress others with your knowledge and erudition. The image that you project is important to your progress now, and your ability to charm those who matter will help you make the grade.

Wednesday, 5th March
Moon conjunct Neptune

The Moon conjuncts Neptune today in a strongly financial area of the chart. Since this influence is dreamy and impressionable, it might not be a good idea to involve yourself with money dealings at the moment. However, in personal relations, the intimacy the conjunction reveals could be tender and loving.

Thursday, 6th March
Moon conjunct Jupiter

Although there might be a test of your self-belief at some point today it's important that you cling to your faith. The Moon conjuncts Jupiter now and lifts your mind out of a rut while setting your sights on affairs in distant parts of the world. You can't be bothered with petty worries and small-minded attitudes. You've got bigger, better concepts to dwell on.

Friday, 7th March
Mars into Virgo retrograde

Mars moves back into your second solar house of finance from today which does put some pressure on your spending power. You have to be sensible for a while and err on the side of caution, because the impulsive nature of the planet will whittle away your resources in no time at all. When money is concerned, keep a tight rein on the cashflow.

Saturday, 8th March
Pluto retrograde

Pluto returns to his old home today for his final visit for two hundred years. At least you won't have to worry about the state of your romances or creative impulses much longer. To be serious, Pluto gives you one last chance to sort out many emotional issues now. It may be that a relationship has come to an end, and if so then part on good terms. Conversely, Pluto could turn a light, no-strings affair into a lasting commitment now.

Sunday, 9th March
New Moon eclipse

The stars are highlighting your direction in life which suggests that you need to think clearly, set goals and then go all out to reach them. Don't allow slower people to hold you back and don't let those who are jealous or resentful of your success put obstacles in your way. It seems to be most important that you forge ahead now while the going is so good.

Monday, 10th March
Sun conjunct Mercury

A free and frank exchange of views is signalled by the conjunction of the Sun and Mercury. In all working situations, from a shop-floor conversation to the most high-powered executive meeting, your views are important. Don't hold back. Raise objections to daft schemes, make sensible suggestions for better practices and more advantageous contracts. You can really do yourself some good by being assertive now. If you're unemployed, there couldn't be a better day to arrange or attend interviews.

Tuesday, 11th March
Moon square Neptune

Don't be led astray by a friend's high-flown ideas today. It's only hot air and you'd be a fool to fall for it. Above all, don't part with any cash on the say-so of your pal. His judgement is flawed to say the least and should not be trusted.

Wednesday, 12th March
Moon square Uranus

Something rather nasty will come out of the woodwork today, and the chances are that a woman will be behind it. You may be the subject of gossip or you could simply be on the receiving end of someone else's spiteful tongue. Your beliefs may be questioned and you could even find yourself accused of being prejudiced.

Thursday, 13th March
Moon sextile Sun

Your mood is calm and you seem content to go along with what others want today. Fortunately, others seem to want much the same as you do, so there shouldn't be any conflicts of interests now.

Friday, 14th March
Moon opposite Pluto
Today has more than its fair share of problems, yet with a methodical attitude and a little determination you'll work your way through them all. There's a conflict between duty and pleasure now, and for once duty seems to come out on top. A difficult task may have to be finished before you can allow yourself quality time. If that's the case then get on with it – the sooner started, the sooner finished. A friend may also need your shoulder to cry on.

Saturday, 15th March
Moon square Venus
You'd love some quiet relaxation today but some well-meaning friends will be determined to drag you kicking and screaming from your shell. It won't matter that you'd like some solitude, or even some intimate time alone with a special person, because your friends have decided that the social scene is where you belong. You'll have to be firm about this, because subtle hints won't work.

Sunday, 16th March
Mercury into Aries
The swift-moving planet, Mercury, enters your eleventh solar house today and gives a remarkable uplift to your social prospects. During the next few weeks you'll find yourself at the centre of friendly interactions. People will seek you out for the pleasure of your company. It's also a good time to get in contact with distant friends and those you haven't seen for a while. The only fly in the ointment is a large 'phone bill!

Monday, 17th March
Sun opposite Mars
Being such a hard worker, you realise how difficult it can

be to maintain the cash for your lifestyle, so it will be easy to become angered by the spendthrift attitude of some people around you today. You may find that so-called friends are all too willing to spend your money while retaining their own by claiming they are broke. Don't stand for any nonsense now. Put your foot down and refuse to supplement extravagance.

Tuesday, 18th March
Moon opposite Neptune

This is not a good day to get involved in any kind of money matter. Don't gamble today and don't agree to any kind of joint venture that involves money. Don't lend money to anyone today, either. Try not to buy anything important or to sign anything important today either, because it will turn out to be an expensive mistake.

Wednesday, 19th March
Moon opposite Uranus

You'll feel that your partner is irritable and difficult today, but if you ask them, they'll say it is you! I think the problem here is one of communication. Are there worries and major issues that are not being discussed in your household? If that's the case then you should put it right at once. There may be a confrontation, but at least it will clear the air and put your relationship back on course.

Thursday, 20th March
Sun into Aries

As the Sun makes its yearly entrance into your eleventh solar house, you can be sure that friends and acquaintances are going to have a powerful influence on your prospects. The Sun's harmonious angle to your own sign gives an optimism and vitality to your outgoing nature. Social life will increase in importance over the next month, and you'll be a popular and much sought-after person. Obstacles that have irritated you will now be swept away.

Friday, 21st March
Mercury conjunct Saturn

Those involved in educational pursuits will do best under today's lunar conjunction with Saturn, since it promotes both concentration and patience. Those who are travelling may experience delays and irritations along the way. Legal and contractual affairs need careful thought before you proceed with any action.

Saturday, 22nd March
Mercury sextile Jupiter

The normal routine of life holds little appeal today for Jupiter and Mercury stimulate an interest far away from your usual activities. If you get the chance, then travel. Both these planets open doorways of opportunity for fun, new experience and adventure. If you can drag a friend along, so much the better because you'll enjoy the company as much as the sightseeing.

Sunday, 23rd March
Venus into Aries

Venus moves into your eleventh house of friendship and group activities today, bringing a few weeks of happiness and harmony for you and your friends. You could fall in love under this transit or you could reaffirm your feelings towards a current partner. You should be looking and feeling rather good now but if not, this is a good time to spend some money on your appearance and also to do something about any nagging health problems.

Monday, 24th March
Full Moon eclipse

Today's eclipse casts a shadow over your sense of fun and frivolity. Life may seem too serious to be bothered with flippant activities or people. A serious attitude will prevail but this shouldn't get you down. Nothing has really changed, so your mood should soon lighten up.

Tuesday, 25th March
Moon opposite Mercury

You may be set on having fun with your friends, but try not to overload your already stretched schedule. Practical affairs have to be dealt with whether you're in the mood or not. We know you want to party, but you'll only end up over-tired and edgy. It may be a case of all work and no play, but it's better in the long run. Resist friends who insist that you be sociable. That's only replacing one duty with another.

Wednesday, 26th March
Moon square Neptune

Common sense flies out of the window today because your heart definitely rules your head. If you've got the urge to express your love by means of an extravagant gesture, please make sure that it's not going to cripple your bank balance.

Thursday, 27th March
Moon square Jupiter

Today, caution should be your watchword. We know that you have been feeling quite optimistic lately, but you also have to keep your feet on the ground. In a work or health situation, listen to the words of a friend who has your welfare at heart.

Friday, 28th March
Moon conjunct Pluto

Some kind of real change is taking place in connection with one particular relationship, and things may never be quite the same again. It looks as if this is a change for the better, so even if you do decide to break with someone now, the outcome will prove to be the right one. You must transform the way you deal with others and turn difficult partnerships into workable ones now.

Saturday, 29th March
Moon trine Venus

Those of you who are alone would do well to get out and about today, because there is definitely something in the air. A friend may introduce you to a potential mate or you may make new friends now who may turn into lovers at a later date. Those of you who are happily settled will enjoy the company of your partner and also of good friends later on today.

Sunday, 30th March
Sun sextile Uranus

The appeal of leaving your daily cares behind you is very strong this Easter Sunday. The Sun makes contact with the restless planet Uranus, which sets your feet tapping with impatience to be up and away. Since this aspect is a good one, you can expect an opportunity to escape the routine. For the very fortunate, a trip abroad is indicated. You need some novelty, and today should inject some into your life.

Monday, 31st March
Sun conjunct Saturn

This is a strange day on which you may find yourself running into old friends or people you used to work with in the past, and this will take you down a path of reminiscence and happy memories. There could be another equally odd event that propels you into the future in a big way. You could meet new people and make new friends who will have a strong influence on your future ideas and decisions. A day to remember.

April at a Glance

LOVE	♥	♥	♥		
WORK	★				
MONEY	$	$	$	$	
FITNESS	⊗	⊗			
LUCK	⋃	⋃	⋃		

Tuesday, 1st April
Mercury into Taurus

You'll find yourself in a more introspective mood for a few weeks because Mercury, planet of the mind, enters the most secret and inward looking portion of your horoscope from today. This is the start of a period when you'll want to understand your own desires and motivations. Too much of a hectic social life will prove a distraction now, so go by instinct and seek out solitude when you feel like it.

Wednesday, 2nd April
Sun conjunct Venus

A friendship that has built up in a professional environment will be worth its weight in gold now, since a favour will come your way just because you are liked.

Women in the workplace are powerfully placed to help you out, and the goodwill of colleagues and bosses will aid your progress no end. Diplomatically you'll chart a course to high achievement now.

Thursday, 3rd April
Sun sextile Jupiter

It may be a Thursday, but social life and celebrations should still be the focus. It doesn't matter if you have to travel some distance to meet up with your friends, because the journey will be worth it. You may even see another, fascinating side to someone you thought you knew well. A profound expression of wisdom will renew your interest.

Friday, 4th April
Moon sextile Mercury

Your mind is working much more clearly than it has been lately and you will soon begin to see answers to some of your problems. You may need to negotiate something at work or ask for something more subtle, such as being treated with respect and understanding by others. You need to behave in a totally professional manner, rather than project a lackadaisical image.

Saturday, 5th April
Moon opposite Mars

In all financial dealings it is wise to be prudent. The lunar opposition to Mars will incline you to be rather free with your cash, whether you've got any or not! If you aren't careful you'll end up providing treats for everyone around you, with no hope of reward.

Sunday, 6th April
Moon trine Pluto

Children will take up much of your time today and you

could learn a few surprising truths. It's about time that some childlike wonder was reintroduced into your life. And, if you can manage to see the world through a youngster's eyes, you'll be that the universe is a truly marvellous place.

Monday, 7th April
New Moon

There's no doubt that issues surrounding friendship and trust are very important now. The New Moon in your horoscopic area of social activities ensures that encounters with interesting people will yield new and enduring friendships. Although your mood has tended to vary between optimism and despair recently, the New Moon can't fail to increase your confidence and vitality.

Tuesday, 8th April
Mercury square Uranus

Too much thinking can be bad for you! Especially when you dwell on old disappointments, hurts and failures. If you aren't careful you'll persuade yourself that you are totally worthless. Nothing could be further from the truth!

Wednesday, 9th April
Moon trine Mars

Today is a good day for work on or in the home, so if you want to get some decorating or other chores done, now is the time for it. You and your partner should be in a cheerful and happy frame of mind but neither of you will feel much like socialising today. You seem to be happy just to be together as much as possible just now.

Thursday, 10th April
Moon trine Neptune

Your mind is turning inwards at the moment and you

might be concentrating on things that are outside your normal routine. You may find yourself thinking of such things as religion, the occult or even the more serious aspects of astrology for a while. Artistic or creative subjects may inspire you now and you could start a new project, go along to a gallery or listen to some good music today.

Friday, 11th April
Moon trine Jupiter

With the added encouragement of Jupiter in your house of adventure and travel, the Moon urges movement in your life. This is not a day to sit at home knitting. Get out and about, meet people, go sightseeing. In short, anything that gives a new experience is favoured now. If you don't feel that you can just take off, then open a good book or watch an interesting documentary. The mind needs some expansion, so give it the chance.

Saturday, 12th April
Moon sextile Venus

There's the prospect of some new faces in your life today. If you're invited to any social gathering you'd better make up your mind to go, because you'll certainly miss out if you don't attend. If by some chance no invitations are forthcoming, then invite your friends to a local bar or club. Good company is vital to you now. You need to feel part of a close-knit group for your personality to shine.

Sunday, 13th April
Moon sextile Mercury

You know that the spotlight is your natural home, and today you'll certainly be the centre of attention since your charisma has gone into overdrive. You're bound to be in demand today, and if you should deign to attend a gathering of friends you'll find that you attract admiration easily. Popularity can't be bought, so the attitude of those around you is a tribute to your personality.

Monday, 14th April
Moon square Sun

Boredom is your big problem today and you'll be tempted to lift yourself out of your languor by digging into your pocket for a good night out or the odd treat or two. Breaking the bank isn't your intention, so don't go mad with the cash card. A demanding child may nag you to provide a toy or fashion item that'll hold their attention for all of five minutes, so don't give in.

Tuesday, 15th April
Mercury retrograde

It is never very comfortable when Mercury travels in retrograde motion and today it turns backwards for the next two or three weeks. Try not to agree to anything important during this phase and also try not to get involved in arguments with colleagues or neighbours. Get the car serviced if necessary but be sure to check that the garage has done all that they are charging you for.

Wednesday, 16th April
Venus into Taurus

As Venus enters your solar house of secrets and psychology, it's obvious that the next few weeks will increase the importance of discretion in your romantic life. You'll find that it'll be wise to draw a veil over the more intimate side of your nature, and you'll be less inclined to confide your deepest secrets even to your closest friends. Quiet interludes with the one you love will be far more attractive than painting the town red just now.

Thursday, 17th April
Moon trine Sun

Popularity is the keyword of the day and a cheery smile and a few moments spent in conversation will restore your perspective on life. You'll be sought after for the pleasure of your company. This is a lucky day, but don't bite off more than you can chew simply because everything's going so well. You'll end up with a mountain of unfinished duties . . . and it's a different story tomorrow.

Friday, 18th April
Moon trine Mercury

You won't be able to complain about being kept in the dark today because there seem to be messages, letters, phone calls and faxes coming at you from all directions. You may need to attend to paperwork or to details of some kind at your place of work. Try to keep all these bits of paper together in one place (especially those that relate to money) because they may get lost.

Saturday, 19th April
Sun square Neptune

You'll be full of big ideas and fanciful schemes today, but we doubt that financial realities will allow you to get any of them off the ground. Be particularly careful if you are trying to take out loans. There are many pitfalls in financial dealings.

Sunday, 20th April
Sun into Taurus

The Sun moves into Taurus today, making you very aware of your inner world of dreams and imagination. For the next month you'll sense the hurdles that face you, and all those things that tend to restrict your freedom. However, your imagination and almost psychic insight will provide the necessary clues to overcome these obstacles. Issues of privacy are very important for the next few weeks.

Monday, 21st April
Mercury square Uranus

You'll be prone to a lot of self-doubt today, but you shouldn't give in to it. My feeling is that you need some lively company to take you out of this introspective mood.

Tuesday, 22nd April
Full Moon

Something is coming to a head in relation to your work. This is not a major crisis and there is absolutely no need to flounce out of a perfectly good job, but there is a problem that should be solved before you can continue on in a happy and peaceful frame of mind. You may have to sort out what your role is and which part of the job other people should be doing, because it looks as if you are carrying too much of the load at the moment.

Wednesday, 23rd April
Venus square Uranus

Your love life or lack of it could provide some problems today. You may be feeling ignored or taken for granted. Don't worry, this phase will soon pass and youll be back to your old self in no time at all.

Thursday, 24th April
Moon square Jupiter

There's nothing you'd like better than to jet off to the sun, to escape boring drudgery and the mind-numbing routine of life. Unfortunately, you are likely to feel more bored before you can break out of this mood.

Friday, 25th April
Sun conjunct Mercury

The Sun and Mercury move into close conjunction today which heightens your imagination to the point of pain. It will be too easy to get carried away with an idea and let baseless fears rule your life. You're quite emotional now, so when the light of reason is overwhelmed by your desires, your anxieties come to the fore. Don't be taken in by flights of fancy.

Saturday, 26th April
Moon sextile Jupiter

You and your lover seem to be happy to do things together today. You are both on the same wavelength now and your dreams and ideas seem to be much the same as each other's.

Sunday, 27th April
Mars direct

You have had to put a good many plans aside lately, especially in connection with your home and family, but the planets are suggesting that you get these plans out of storage once again and put them into action. It may be that you have discarded some ideas as being unworkable, but now there will be an opportunity to find others and to put them into operation. Your energy levels will be higher from now on too.

Monday, 28th April
Sun square Uranus

Prepare to be astounded! You may want nothing more than a quiet day but the world at large is equally determined that you aren't going to get one. The 'phone will continuously ring, and people will demand your attention. Well, it's better than being unpopular!

Tuesday, 29th April
Moon square Mercury

You could be having some kind of crisis of conscience today because you are finding it hard to go along with the beliefs or the behaviour of others. If others insist on breaking the law or behaving in a particularly spiteful or nasty manner to a third party, then keep yourself right out of the situation and do what you know to be right. Keep to the straight and narrow and you can't go wrong.

Wednesday, 30th April
Venus trine Mars

The combination of Venus and Mars hints at romance, especially if it happens to be of the clandestine variety. In fact secrets of all kinds are revealed by today's stars and it could be that an old skeleton is rattling in your family's closet.

May at a Glance

LOVE	♥	♥	♥	♥	
WORK	★	★			
MONEY	$	$	$	$	
FITNESS	◓	◓			
LUCK	∪	∪	∪		

Thursday, 1st May
Neptune retrograde

Neptune turns to retrograde motion today and that will

bring a few muddles and misunderstandings in connection with money and partnerships. This is a bad time to get involved with other people in any kind of business arrangement and it would be unwise to lend money to anybody. This is also not a good time to get involved sexually with anybody, especially if you don't know them very well!

Friday, 2nd May
Venus square Jupiter

Although you're much in demand socially, you'll be in no mood to stick to one person or topic for very long today. Those two beneficial planets, Venus and Jupiter, successfully increase your charm but also add a wicked element of flirtation and teasing. At least this will give you a very alluring and enigmatic aura. Foreigners or news from abroad will be a feature of the day.

Saturday, 3rd May
Mercury square Neptune

Some gossip that you hear today will be totally inaccurate, so don't put any credence in it at all. The intimate lives of those we know are often a source of fascination, but this particular juicy snippet is pure fiction, so don't spread it any further!

Sunday, 4th May
Moon conjunct Saturn

Now you will really find out who your friends are because you will have the strength to confront anyone who you suspect has been less than a good friend to you, in order to sort out a drama that has been building up. There may be some really good news in connection with older members of the family or about people who hold positions of responsibility. You could also have a good day in some kind of group activity.

Monday, 5th May
Mercury into Aries retrograde

Mercury's return visit to your solar house of friendships and hopes suggests that an old acquaintance will be soon coming back into your life. Apart from that, a dream you once had and then dismissed could now be seen as more feasible.

Tuesday, 6th May
New Moon

The world of romance is especially attractive on a day when your dreams and fantasies take over your life. The New Moon points the way to new emotional experiences in the future, but you mustn't cling to the past because of misplaced loyalty or guilt. Some people are leaving your life, but if you are honest you'll admit that they're no real loss. Follow your instincts now and your dreams may well come true.

Wednesday, 7th May
Sun trine Mars

Some big plans may have to be put on hold for a while simply because you haven't got the cash resources to back them up. That is the sensible solution, but we doubt that you'll be too keen for any delay to creep into your well thought-out schemes. Therefore you're likely to be very active today looking for alternative sources of finance. Self-employed people will have considerable ingenuity in dealing with accountants and banks.

Thursday, 8th May
Mercury direct

If you've not been seeing eye-to-eye with certain friends recently, you can put the blame on Mercury's wayward course which has made all social relations that much more difficult recently. Fortunately, the tiny planet is now moving along the right road so it's time to pour oil on troubled waters and re-establish the friendly social links you previously enjoyed.

Friday, 9th May
Moon trine Jupiter

This is a great day to take a chance on anything. If you are fond of a wager, try your luck now. Don't get carried away and bet more than you can afford, but a really small wager would be fun, and it should come up trumps. Someone may suggest that you take a long-distance trip, and this too looks well starred. You may decide to learn something new now and this will go well, especially if the subject is an unusual one.

Saturday, 10th May
Venus into Gemini

The luxury-loving planet, Venus, is suggesting that this is a great time to spoil and enjoy yourself. So treat yourself to something nice and new that is for you alone. A new outfit would be a good idea, or a few nice-smelling toiletries. Throw a party for your favourite friends and don't turn your head and look the other way if someone seems to be fancying you.

Sunday, 11th May
Sun square Jupiter

The mundane duties expected of you today seem far too heavy a burden. The smallest task becomes a mammoth bind, and you resent the intrusion into your inner world. Don't build molehills into mountains today; just take it as it comes.

Monday, 12th May
Mercury into Taurus

You may receive a surprise letter or 'phone call from someone whom you had relegated to the background of your life. Another possibility is that you will have to spend the next couple of weeks sorting out some kind of outstanding paperwork or even a muddle related to your work. This is a good time to put right any misunderstandings and even to apologise to someone if you feel that you owe them this.

Tuesday, 13th May
Uranus retrograde

Uranus turns to retrograde motion today and this will bring some delays and setbacks in various areas of your life over the next few weeks. You may find it difficult to fit in travel plans with other members of the family, or these may clash with your job or with other duties that you have to perform. You may wish to escape from the chores, only to find that you can't. There could be legal or official problems to contend with over the next few weeks as well.

Wednesday, 14th May
Venus opposite Pluto

Venus's opposition to Pluto shows that change is imminent in close personal relationships. You may find that your heart lies elsewhere or that a deeper commitment is now required that will change the way you live your life. Your heart rules your head at the moment and you have little choice but to follow its dictates.

Thursday, 15th May
Moon square Venus

Whatever gender you are, you will find the most help and the best company among your female friends and relatives today. You will find it easier to relate to women now and, whether you make time for coffee with your sister or a few drinks in the pub with a dear friend, you'll thank your lucky stars that you have such an understanding and congenial pal to chat to.

Friday, 16th May
Moon conjunct Mars

Something will take you back to revisit your past today. You may bump into an old flame and take time out to talk about times gone by, or you may find yourself back in a part of town that you haven't been near for years. Something may help you to come to terms with old hurts and disappointments for once and all.

Saturday, 17th May
Venus trine Uranus

A female friend or relative will be instrumental in setting you straight and giving you peace of mind. You will soon realise that you are on the right track and that you are not necessarily wrong just because other people seem to see things differently. Travel is very well starred today, as is any kind of trip that takes you on or over water. If you want to be refreshed, take a trip to a river, lake or the sea.

Sunday, 18th May
Moon trine Venus

Your mind will be on romance today, and fate may encourage you to expresses your feelings to your loved one. It is a good day to treat your partner to a small gift, a night out in his or her favourite restaurant, to the theatre or any other treat that he or she would appreciate. You can forget the mundane world for a while today and concentrate on the fun side of life for once.

Monday, 19th May
Moon trine Jupiter

With a good aspect between the Moon and Jupiter there should be a considerable easing of your emotional state. This is a day to breathe a sigh of relief, settle down into an aura of comfort and affection, and generally take it easy. Of course, you tend to be a stranger to quiet relaxation, so involve yourself in an activity that you actually like. A day trip with the one you love is a very good idea.

Tuesday, 20th May
Sun trine Neptune

If you are keen to investigate psychic or occult matters, this is a good time to do so. Your intuitive powers are on a high just now and, if you want to join a seance or learn to be a medium or a spiritual healer, there could hardly be a better time to do so. You may be drawn towards astrology too, especially the more personal kind of astrology where you learn to make up and interpret a birth chart.

Wednesday, 21st May
Sun into Gemini

The Sun moves into your own sign today, bringing with it a lifting of your spirits and a gaining of confidence all round. Your birthday will soon be here and we hope that it will be a good one for you. You may see more of your family than is usual now and there should be some socialising and partying to look forward to. Music belongs to the realm of the Sun, so treat yourself to a musical treat soon.

Thursday, 22nd May
Full Moon

The Full Moon shines in the area of close relationships today. Since it is a stress indicator, you'd be wise to build some bridges within a close partnership now, either that or be content to let an emotional link drift ... possibly away! Your understanding and tolerance will be the key to relationship success now.

Friday, 23rd May
Venus sextile Saturn

If you are single and are keen to meet someone to love, then today's events could be extremely interesting and also very important to you in the long run. The reason for this is that a friend could be instrumental in introducing you to someone who will become part of your future. For those of you who are already in committed relationships, you may make a good new friend today.

Saturday, 24th May
Sun opposite Pluto

There is a great deal of tension around you at the moment and, unfortunately, this situation is simply not going to disappear on its own. You are being faced with having to alter some of your relationships with others in an important way. The good news is that the trouble may not affect your relationship with your lover, but it may well change some of your other relationships.

Sunday, 25th May
Moon square Saturn

You seem afflicted by an aura of gloom today. It's all the fault of the lunar aspect to Saturn which puts a dampner on anything that would usually please you. Money could be the area that you blame most for this grim mood. Brighten up! It can't possibly be as bad as you think!

Monday, 26th May
Moon conjunct Neptune

The lunar conjunction with Neptune puts you in touch with your deepest feelings and instincts today. In all matters requiring an intuitive perception you will excel. From sexual affairs to complex financial dealings, follow your instincts and you won't go wrong.

Tuesday, 27th May
Venus trine Jupiter

It can't fail to be a lucky day when there's such an excellent angle between Jupiter and Venus. These two fortunate planets cast their helpful influence over travel and a deepening of understanding. A love affair that starts now has the most favourable chances. Be adventurous and get out into the world; there's nothing at all to fear.

Wednesday, 28th May
Venus square Mars

Keep your mind on what you are doing in and around the home today. Mars is badly aspected and this could bring silly accidents while working around the place. It is a poor day for getting on with home improvements, decorating, dressmaking or fancy cooking. It will be better to go out or simply to relax and forget the chores for once.

Thursday, 29th May
Sun trine Uranus

You are in an exuberant and quite outrageous mood today. Since you'll be game for a laugh you'll be prepared to shock others out of complacency by pointing out certain flaws in their arguments and highlighting their prejudices.

Though this will be for the best possible reasons, you'll enjoy rupturing their pomposity, too!

Friday, 30th May
Moon square Venus

Venus's residence in your sign should be extremely helpful to you, and so it will be, but today there is a slight hiccup in all this. Women may be irritating to deal with, and someone may try to run you down either to your face or behind your back. This could be quite serious because it could temporarily block your progress in at least one important area of your life.

Saturday, 31st May
Moon sextile Uranus

If you have been trying to put things right between you and your friends or if you have been putting up with some kind of unpleasantness from one, so called, friend, then the events of today will help to put things right. Another person, perhaps outside your actual circle, may be just the right person to help you deal with this. Your philosophy of life is changing now and you will come out of this thinking differently.

June at a Glance

LOVE	♥	♥	♥	♥	♥
WORK	★	★	★		
MONEY	$	$	$	$	$
FITNESS	🫀	🫀	🫀	🫀	🫀
LUCK	☡	☡	☡	☡	☡

Sunday, 1st June
Moon sextile Jupiter

There's no doubt that you are determined to improve your position as far as professional success is concerned, but of course you may feel that some improvement of the mind is also in order. Perhaps a new educational course or an evening class would appeal now. You're such a determined person that you should dismiss any idea that it would be a waste of time. Remember that the energy you expend now will be amply repaid with achievement.

Monday, 2nd June
Moon square Uranus

You and your loved ones may disagree on matters of religion or philosophy. Another possibility is that you will think that what they are saying is crazy, but you seem to want to keep your thoughts firmly to yourself. Perhaps it's better that way! You may have to take an unexpected trip over quite a long distance in connection with an older family member who suddenly finds themselves needing help or support.

Tuesday, 3rd June
Moon conjunct Mercury

Your imagination is very strong and possibly a little too heated today. The Moon unites with Mercury in your solar house of the subconscious, bringing many dreams and fantasies to light. Although these are things that you'd usually be inclined to keep to yourself, you'll be surprised at how easily you can communicate them to someone who understands.

Wednesday, 4th June
Venus into Cancer

Your financial state should experience a welcome boost for a few weeks as Venus, one of the planetary indicators of wealth, moves into your solar house of possessions and economic security from today. You feel that you deserve a lifestyle full of luxury now and this will be reflected in the good taste you express when making purchases for your home. Your sense of self-worth is boosted too which might indicate a renewed interest in high fashion.

Thursday, 5th June
New Moon

Theres a New Moon in your own sign today. This is a powerfully positive influence that encourages you to make a new start. Personal opportunities are about to change your life, and you must now be prepared to leave the past behind to embark on a brand new course. Decide what you want, because you'll be your own best guide now.

Friday, 6th June
Mercury trine Mars

A secret is likely to be confided to you today. It would be in your best interests to keep this piece of information to yourself since it could involve a skeleton in the family closet.

Saturday, 7th June
Sun sextile Saturn

You may feel the need to surround yourself with people who are older and wiser today so that you can benefit from their experience. A serious attitude to life will win the respect of your associates.

Sunday, 8th June
Mercury into Gemini

The movement of Mercury into your own sign signals the start of a period of much clearer thinking for you. You will know where you want to go and what you want to do from now on. It will be quite easy for you to influence others with the brilliance of your ideas and you will also be able to project just the right image. Guard against trying to crowd too much into one day.

Monday, 9th June
Mercury trine Neptune

Your mood is intensely romantic and overwhelmingly sexy today. You may be in the first stages of a new love affair or you may be looking longingly at someone whom you find stupendously attractive. We refuse to dish out sensible advice to you, because you won't be able to take it in! You are probably acting foolishly but we all need to do that from time to time, don't we?

Tuesday, 10th June
Jupiter retrograde

Jupiter turns backward today, so keep your feet on the ground and remember that just because the general outlook is good for you personally it doesn't mean that you don't have to work for it, or get it handed to you on a plate. In many ways you have to make your own luck at the moment, but even so, educational and travel matters may meet with delays and frustrations for a while.

Wednesday, 11th June
Sun trine Jupiter

You have restless feet today. The prospect of summer opens your eyes to everything that the world has to offer. You want to be up and away as soon as possible, so this should be an excellent time to make plans for a much-needed holiday. Friends who are far away may come into your thoughts now, so perhaps you should get in touch.

Thursday, 12th June
Mercury trine Uranus

Mercury is well aspected today and this will keep your 'phone ringing and your post box full. Fortunately, the news should be very good with unexpected invitations and cheering messages from friends. There is even the possibility of an unexpected windfall today. You may have one or two really bright ideas and some of these could include travel plans.

Friday, 13th June
Moon conjunct Mars

This could be another tense day around the home. The lunar conjunction with Mars ensures that tempers are frayed and that feelings are running high. A lot of the fault will lie with you though, simply because you are being rather demanding at the moment and family members are becoming resentful of this tyranny. If you could learn to compromise a little then you'd all get along far better.

Saturday, 14th June
Moon trine Uranus

You seem to be filled with some kind of magical charisma today which will attract the opposite sex like bees to a honey-pot! You may fall head over heels in love with a devastatingly attractive person, or you may find that someone else has fallen crazily in love with you. Your sense of proportion and perspective will go completely and you won't know whether you are coming or going.

Sunday, 15th June
Mars trine Neptune

Whether you are at home or at work today, you will find the world a good place and the people in it easy to get along with. Females could fall deeply and sincerely in love today, while males too could have the kind of romantic day that is hard to forget. Dreams of all kinds could come true and, whether you are looking for success on the sports field or the job of a lifetime, you should be prepared to go all out for it now.

Monday, 16th June
Moon square Neptune

It's not a day to gamble, to take a chance or to reveal secrets! The lunar aspect to Neptune shows that anything covert or even slightly criminal is to be avoided like the plague.

Tuesday, 17th June
Moon trine Venus

If you get stuck into the chores today, you will get them done in no time at all. So, if you have been putting off some boring job either at home or at your place of work, get it out of the way for good and all today. You may push yourself a bit too hard, but we all do this from time to time and today is your day for being the world's greatest workaholic.

Wednesday, 18th June
Mercury sextile Saturn

There's a calm, controlled atmosphere today as you talk over your plans with a close friend. A more mature point of view will go a long way to clarifying certain personal issues now. If you ask for advice, listen to what you receive. It may not be what you want to hear, but you can be sure it's for the best.

Thursday, 19th June
Mars into Libra

Your desires suddenly become very strong indeed as Mars changes sign, and temptations will tend to sweep you up without a single thought for the consequences. If the path of true love doesn't run smoothly, it's not for want of passionate intensity on your part. The one thing to watch for is that you'll tend to move so swiftly that you're prone to minor cuts and bruises . . . so take it easy.

Friday, 20th June
Full Moon

Today's Full Moon puts a lunar spotlight on your physical state. Knowing you, you've been overworking and pushing your system to the very limit. It's now time to be realistic about the stresses that have been imposed upon you, and act accordingly. You may feel the need to take up some form of exercise, or adjust your diet to something more healthy. You have the chance to reject bad habits such as smoking or excessive drinking now. Look after your body!

Saturday, 21st June
Sun into Cancer

Your financial prospects take an upturn from today as the Sun enters your house of money and possessions. The next month should see an improvement in your economic security, and it may be that you need to lay plans to ensure maximum profit now. Don't expect any swift returns for investments, but lay down a pattern for future growth. Sensible monetary decisions made now will pay off in a big way.

Sunday, 22nd June
Sun square Mars

Keep that fiery temper under control today. The Sun's harsh aspect to Mars makes it too easy to blow minor financial concerns out of all proportion. You may even think that you're being reasonable, but unfortunately those around you will know that this is not the case. Try to address worries sensibly rather than taking out your frustrations on those who will support you given half the chance.

Monday, 23rd June
Mercury into Cancer

All the planets seem to be restless just now since Mercury changes sign today. At least you can get your mind into gear concerning the state of your finances now. Tasks you've been putting off, like cancelling useless standing orders or ensuring you receive the most advantageous interest from your savings, will be tackled with ease.

Tuesday, 24th June
Mercury square Mars

There could be considerable tension between you and the younger members of the family now. They may be going that bit too far and taking your good nature for granted or being thoughtless or careless in some way. Ask yourself if what you want of them is reasonable and, if the answer is yes, then insist on it. You may find that your lover doesn't share your priorities today and this could also cause a bit of tension.

Wednesday, 25th June
Sun conjunct Mercury

This is an excellent day on which to pull off a really spectacular deal, so if you feel like wheeling and dealing in the big leagues, then do so today! Even if you are only looking around for something for yourself or your family, you should be able to find just what you want now. This is also the time for buying or selling a vehicle, or for getting one put back into good working order.

Thursday, 26th June
Mars sextile Pluto

The heart will rule the head today, but there's absolutely nothing wrong in that. Ignore the objections of everyone else and do as your feelings bid you. You can't go wrong and you could transform your life in an extremely positive way!

Friday, 27th June
Venus opposite Neptune

Guard against unnecessary spending because anything that you buy now is unlikely to turn out to be much of a bargain. Women may lead you in the wrong direction in some way today, so try to rely upon your own judgement rather than that of your female friends. Women colleagues may be vague and peculiar in some way today.

Saturday, 28th June
Venus into Leo

If you've got any favours to ask, the passage of Venus into your solar house of persuasion shows that you can use considerable charm and eloquence to win others over to your point of view. A little flirtation combined with a winning way ensures that you achieve your desires. Your creative talents are boosted too, so perhaps you should consider writing down your inspirations now.

Sunday, 29th June
Moon square Venus

There are some days when you just want to be left alone with your own thoughts. Unfortunately, your popularity is such that others are anxious for your company. If you really want solitude then you'll have to pretend that you're out. Don't answer the door or the 'phone. Relax, surround yourself with music and sink back into your favourite chair. Alternatively, a long walk in the fresh air will restore your spirits.

Monday, 30th June
Moon sextile Mercury

Keep a few matters to yourself today. Even if a friend or a neighbour tries to worm things out of you, try to keep your mouth firmly shut. Your financial position is improving rapidly now but it would be a good idea to keep quiet, because there are plenty of people around you who would be only too happy to cash in on your hard-earned pennies.

July at a Glance

LOVE	♥	♥	♥	♥	
WORK	★	★	★	★	★
MONEY	$	$	$	$	$
FITNESS	◓	◓	◓	◓	◓
LUCK	♘	♘	♘	♘	♘

Tuesday, 1st July
Venus trine Pluto
If you are thinking of popping the question (or waiting for the question to be popped!) this could be the day. The romance of Venus unites with the sultry passion of Pluto, showing that intimate feelings are about to be expressed.

Wednesday, 2nd July
Mercury square Saturn
You seem to be fighting an uphill battle with a group of people, but you cannot simply walk away and forget it. Your friends may be unable or unwilling to understand your position or to help you out of a spot now. It is absolutely no good sitting still and dreaming – you must take a practical view of things and get down to doing something about it. You could have to discard some unwanted goods now.

Thursday, 3rd July
Venus sextile Mars
It is absolutely necessary for you to keep up with all the news and gossip that is flying around today, because that

is the only way you will be able to keep on top of your situation. There seem to be a number of changes occurring now, so for your own sake you should make quite sure that you're kept completely up to date.

Friday, 4th July
New Moon

Today's New Moon shows that your financial affairs have reached a point where you have to make a decision. Do you carry on in the old, and rather dreary ways of making and spending your cash or should you look at the realities and make sensible decisions? This isn't a time to retreat into dreamland, or to carry on with bad budgeting. Look at your monetary state carefully.

Saturday, 5th July
Venus opposite Uranus

Feelings run high today and harsh words are likely to be spoken. An unexpected reaction to an idle comment will lead you to the conclusion that the emotional under-currents run very deep indeed. Tread carefully!

Sunday, 6th July
Mars trine Uranus

Forget duty and go with the flow today. If the chance arises for a journey in congenial company, then go at once. You're bound to have a fantastic time.

Monday, 7th July
Mercury opposite Neptune

Lock away your cheque book, hide your credit cards and keep away from the shops. Money is likely to slip through your fingers like water today if you aren't careful. This wouldn't be so bad if you had something to show for it, but unfortunately you're unlikely to get anything of real value for your cash.

Tuesday, 8th July
Mercury into Leo

Your mind will be going full-speed ahead over the next few weeks and you are bound to come up with some really great new ideas. You will be very busy with the 'phone constantly ringing and letters falling through your letter box by the ton. You will find yourself acting as a temporary secretary for a while, even if the only person who makes use of your services is you.

Wednesday, 9th July
Mercury trine Pluto

Relationship problems should be solved easily today, since you are extra perceptive and able to approach the most delicate subject with tact and diplomacy. You can reassure your partner and soothe fears with a few well-chosen words now.

Thursday, 10th July
Moon trine Neptune

There's a touch of deception around at the moment, and you can't blame anyone but yourself. Gossip is rife and the rumours all add up to a totally wrong conclusion. In other words, two and two don't make five! If you're concerned about your security and the future solvency of a firm, don't fly into a panic just yet. Your fears are likely to be unfounded.

Friday, 11th July
Sun square Saturn

You are definitely up against it at the moment, and the issue seems to be about respect and authority. Thus, you may find yourself being badly treated by someone in authority or by someone who is unwilling to show you a reasonable amount of respect for what you do. Or, you may be demanding too much of others, and you will have to ask yourself whether you are being reasonable or not.

Saturday, 12th July
Moon sextile Venus

A long chat to a woman friend is just what you need to get your life into perspective. Talking over old times, or indeed times to come, a gossip and a laugh will set you up for anything the world could possibly throw at you.

Sunday, 13th July
Moon square Neptune

Don't enter into any hire-purchase or loan agreements today! Your view of your spending power is somewhat distorted by wishful thinking. The cold light of common sense is not to be seen today, so be extra careful with all your cash.

Monday, 14th July
Jupiter sextile Saturn

The excellent aspect between Jupiter and Saturn urges you to forget self-imposed limitations and to strike out on a new and more challenging course. If you are academically-minded, then this aspect predicts immense success for your intellectual efforts.

Tuesday, 15th July
Mercury sextile Mars

You may visit family members today or you could be on the receiving end of visits from relatives now. Sisters, brothers and grown children may drop in on you, so make sure that you have some extra food in stock just in case.

There could be good news in connection with relatives or to do with a business matter that is in hand just now.

Wednesday, 16th July
Moon sextile Uranus

There could be some really unexpected news from overseas or from someone who lives at a distance from you now. Fortunately, the news is good and this will allay any fears that you may have had about your distant friend or relative's welfare. For some of you, love could come in to your life and it could be a fascinating foreigner or someone from a different culture who makes your heart pound so.

Thursday, 17th July
Moon trine Saturn

A suggestion made by your spouse or a close friend should be heeded today. This comment will have a wealth of common sense behind it, and it is not something that you can afford to ignore.

Friday, 18th July
Mercury opposite Jupiter

Gemini people are often stubborn, so opposition to your views is nothing new to you. Today however, the opposition between Mercury and Jupiter shows that you aren't really prepared for the tenacity with which others hold to their opinions. You can't win an argument now; those around you will only dig in their heels, so try to avoid confrontation.

Saturday, 19th July
Moon square Saturn

An old friend may leave your life soon. However, this parting need not be permanent even though you will feel a keen sense of loss.

Sunday, 20th July
Full Moon

The Full Moon brings to the surface intense feelings that you have buried away in some vault of memory. You'll be forced to look at yourself stripped bare of illusions now. That's not such a bad thing, because you'll realise that many of your hang-ups have been a total waste of time and should be ditched. You may have a financial worry coming to a head so today's aspect encourages you to take decisive action to sort it out once and for all.

Monday, 21st July
Sun opposite Neptune

This is likely to be a rather grim day on the financial scene. The Sun is opposed to Neptune which is not a good situation for your cashflow. Overspending is likely or you become aware of the consequences of past indulgence. Be careful that you don't make plans without being able to fund them.

Tuesday, 22nd July
Sun into Leo

Your curiosity will be massively stimulated from today as the Sun enters the area of learning and communication. Other people's business suddenly becomes your own. That's not to say that you turn into a busybody overnight, it's just that many will turn to you for some guidance. Affairs in the lives of your brothers, sisters and neighbours have extra importance now. Short journeys too are well starred for one month.

Wednesday, 23rd July
Venus into Virgo

Old scores and family squabbles can now be laid to rest as the passage of Venus into your domestic area signals a time of harmony and contentment. Surround yourself with beauty, both in terms of affection and in material possessions. This is a good time to renew a closeness with those you love. Join forces to complete a major project such as redecoration, or even a move of home itself. Be assured that the stars smile on you now.

Thursday, 24th July
Moon trine Pluto

Relationships of all kinds will go very smoothly today and you may decide that this is the time to deepen a commitment. Friends could be instrumental in helping you to sort out some part of your life that has become muddled, and this could result in your having a much clearer idea of what you want from others. You may transform a relationship in some way.

Friday, 25th July
Venus square Pluto

A home-based project or a desire you have to make a new and rather expensive purchase for your home will not find favour with your other half today. If you don't want to cause fireworks, the pair of you had better agree to disagree on this topic!

Saturday, 26th July
Mars trine Jupiter

There's a tremendous boost to your physical and mental energies today as Mars enters a superb angle with the expansive Jupiter. Optimism, vivacity and a lust for life are the gifts of this powerful stellar influence. You'll be outgoing, exuberant and playful now. Both the romantic area of your life and travel affairs will benefit.

Sunday, 27th July
Mercury into Virgo

The past exerts a powerful influence as Mercury enters the house of heritage. You'll find that things long forgotten will somehow re-enter your life over the next couple of weeks. An interest in your family heritage may develop, or possibly a new-found passion for antiques. Some good, meaningful conversations in the family will prove enlightening.

Monday, 28th July
Mars opposite Saturn

It's likely to be a trying day in terms of love affairs and friendships. You won't be in tune with anyone at all at the moment, and your irritable attitudes could easily cause arguments.

Tuesday, 29th July
Sun opposite Uranus

Unusual and unexpected news will have you scuttling hither and thither at a moment's notice. You may decide to take a sudden trip abroad or to do something drastic about changing your usual mode of transport. Something that a friend says to you could make you change your usual way of looking at life. You will begin to look at yourself as well as your surrounding world in a very different way.

Wednesday, 30th July
Moon trine Mars

Children or young people in your circle will bring you a great deal of pleasure today, either because they make some kind of achievement or simply because you all enjoy doing things together. This would be a great day for playing a nice game of golf, football, cricket or anything else that you fancy. In short, anything that gets you out into the open air and gives you a break from routine.

Thursday, 31st July
Moon sextile Mercury

This is an excellent time to invest in property or to take on some kind of extra premises. You may want to enlarge or improve your home, or acquire or rent out a business property. Brothers, sisters and neighbours could become involved in your plans.

August at a Glance

LOVE	♥	♥	♥		
WORK	★	★	★		
MONEY	$				
FITNESS	⏺				
LUCK	☋	☋			

Friday, 1st August
Saturn retrograde

A number of areas of your life will tend to slow down for a while and, in addition to this, you will find yourself having to take on more responsibility. You may find yourself in charge of some kind of group connected with work or some part of your social life. If you have to guide and influence others now, you may have to do so the hard way – by putting your foot down.

Saturday, 2nd August
Moon trine Pluto

You and your partner should have no difficulty communicating with each other today. You may be able to clear the air and get a better idea of what your other half is feeling. There could be good news concerning joint financial matters, and it is possible that your partner could be doing better than he or she had anticipated.

Sunday, 3rd August
New Moon

The New Moon shows a change in your way of thinking. In many ways you'll know that it's time to move on. Perhaps you'll find yourself in a new company, a new home or among a new circle of friends in the near future. Opinions are set to change as you are influenced by more stimulating people. Perhaps you'll consider taking up an educational course of some kind.

Monday, 4th August
Moon sextile Mars

It seems that the theme for this week is fun. Today, the Moon and Mars continue the social trend, mixing in a little romantic passion for good measure. This is a day to circulate amongst people you like and respect. You never know, a friendship may deepen into something more intimate before very long.

Tuesday, 5th August
Moon conjunct Mercury

Your home is likely to be the meeting place for half your neighbourhood today. You may decide to throw a party or it may simply be that everybody seem to congregate in your kitchen. News will flow as quickly as the drinks (or the tea and coffee) and the atmosphere will be light and cheerful.

Wednesday, 6th August
Moon conjunct Venus

This should be a good day for your family and your home life. Relatives may pop in with offers of help and useful gifts. Any family get-together now will be extremely successful. This is a good time to buy something beautiful or valuable for your home, arrange for refurbishment or to pick up collectors' items such as antiques or objects d'art.

Thursday, 7th August
Moon sextile Pluto

This is an extremely important day for personal relationships. You may meet someone who changes your life in some way now, or you may begin to realise that someone you thought of as no more than a friend really matters to you. You may do some kind of minor business deal with someone else and, if so, this will go well for both of you. Your dealings seem to be honest and above board, so luck should follow you in whatever you do now.

Friday, 8th August
Moon sextile Sun

It's a day for simple pleasures and innocent enjoyment. A quiet conversation with a child or younger person should show you that you can still learn a thing or two, and have a laugh as well.

Saturday, 9th August
Sun opposite Jupiter

Although you are quite forward-looking and confident today, you may not receive the support you expect from relatives. In fact, you could feel somewhat let down by their negative attitudes to your aspirations and ideas. Don't let this apparent coldness deceive you, for your relations have important concerns of their own and are preoccupied. Concentrate on inner strength; you've got plenty of it!

Sunday, 10th August
Mars square Neptune

Being too hasty with money would be a big mistake today! You might think that you can comfortably afford to indulge a hobby but the true, and possibly hidden, costs will be enormous. Think again!

Monday, 11th August
Moon square Sun

You are going to spend a lot of time on the 'phone over the next month or so and you will also have a pile of correspondence to deal with. This may be the time to get to grips with a new computer program or some other kind of new technology. The age of the horse and cart and the quill pen is definitely over for you now, and you must get 'with-it' in order to cope with the modern world.

Tuesday, 12th August
Sun trine Saturn

You will be able to get your point of view across today in no uncertain terms. You may be involved with powerful and important people but you will not be nervous in their presence. You know that you are in possession of all the relevant facts and that they will trust and believe you. You could be dealing with personal matters, but it is equally possible that you will speak on behalf of a group.

Wednesday, 13th August
Pluto direct

Any partnership matters that have been held up in the works will get moving very quickly now. Depending upon your personal circumstances, this means that you could get contracts or joint ventures off the ground now, or that you and a lover can look forward to a happy future with more confidence. You may find yourself dealing with legal or professional people now and the outcome of this should be good.

Thursday, 14th August
Mars into Scorpio

The transit of Mars into your area of health and work says that you must show that you have initiative and drive to make the most out of your prospects now. The energies of the fiery planet won't allow you to sink anonymously into a crowd. You'll be forced to stand out and make your mark on the professional world. In health affairs, the vitality of the planet must be good news; rarely have you felt so alive and effective. You may find that some colleagues are distressed at this assertion of your personality and aims but, unfortunately for them, they'll just have to put up with it!

Friday, 15th August
Venus trine Neptune

If you are in a settled relationship, you should be getting on better now than you have ever done before. It is just possible that some of you will be going in the opposite direction to the planets now and considering ending your current situation, but for those of you who are settled and happy, you should soon feel even happier.

Saturday, 16th August
Venus into Libra

This is a good day to begin new projects and to get great ideas off the ground. Venus is now moving into the area of your chart that is concerned with creativity, so over the next few weeks you can take advantage of this and get involved with some kind of creative process. Venus is concerned with the production of beauty, so utilise this planetary energy to enhance any of your ventures now.

Sunday, 17th August
Mercury retrograde

Whenever Mercury moves into retrograde motion, life becomes difficult for a while. Therefore over the next few weeks you can expect to be subject to a number of delays and frustrations. People who owe you money may delay payment, letters could go missing in the post and travel plans will be awkward and muddled. You may find it hard to get on with others and your nerves may be on edge.

Monday, 18th August
Full Moon

You may have to face the fact that you cannot slope off to distant and romantic shores just now. This doesn't mean that you are forever confined to your home, just that you cannot get away right now. Your mood is not only escapist but also rebellious today! You won't want to have anything to do with people who restrict you or who remind you of your chores and duties, but you simply won't be able to escape them.

Tuesday, 19th August
Moon opposite Mercury

You may have to rush round to see one or other of your parents today. Alternatively, another older member of your circle could need your assistance now. The problem is that the messages that you are being given are a bit muddled and, when you actually look into the reality of the situation, it may be much better than you first realised.

Wednesday, 20th August
Moon sextile Neptune

Your sensitive handling of a delicate situation will find favour with bosses and other authority figures today. This could be an opportunity for career advancement or a rise of some kind.

Thursday, 21st August
Venus trine Uranus

You will be full of bright ideas which will, fortunately, turn out to be quite practical when you put them to the test. A woman friend or relative will surprise you by taking you out to see or do something interesting. You may enjoy a mild but quite disturbing flirtation today, and this could have the effect of making you feel restless and uncertain about your usual partnerships or relationships.

Friday, 22nd August
Mars square Uranus

If what you want is a nice restful day, filled with such activities as soaking in a scented bath, watching your favourite sport on the television or enjoying a leisurely round of golf, then you are out of luck! This is going to be a hectic day with many unexpected events and even a catastrophe or two for you to deal with. Most likely, you will be chasing about like crazy and probably getting nowhere fast.

Saturday, 23rd August
Sun into Virgo

The home and family become your main interest over the next four weeks as the Sun moves into the most domestic area of your chart from today. Family feuds will now be resolved, and you'll find an increasing contentment in your own surroundings. A haven of peace will be restored in your home. This should also be a period of nostalgia when happy memories come flooding back.

Sunday, 24th August
Moon trine Neptune

Unseen forces seem to be working in your favour now and you could find yourself getting on much better in life than for some time past. You may have friends in high places who are beavering away on your behalf now. You could just as easily attract the attention of a new and exciting lover, simply by being in the right place at the right time. The message here is that you don't have to work hard at anything to make it happen today.

Monday, 25th August
Sun square Pluto

Trying to get your own way by playing the tyrant in your family circle won't get you very far, but it could serve a purpose as an excuse to let off some steam. Don't go too far though, or you could set up resentments that will last for ages.

Tuesday, 26th August
Moon sextile Saturn

A serious discussion with a friend will show that you aren't the flippant person that you often pretend to be. You will understand your friend's circumstances simply because you've been in the same position previously.

Wednesday, 27th August
Moon sextile Sun

This is an excellent day on which to buy goodies for the home. So, if your curtains need replacing or if the dog has chewed the cushion covers just one time too many, take yourself out to the shops and see what you can do about it.

Thursday, 28th August
Venus trine Jupiter

The fortunate influence of Jupiter combines with Venus now, making this a day to remember. Love, happiness, luck and optimism are the gifts of these two most beneficial planets. Links with someone of a different national or ethnic background could develop in a romantic way. Children too could encourage you to look at the world positively. This is a deeply fulfilling time.

Friday, 29th August
Mercury sextile Mars

You seem to be up to your neck in chores today, and you may feel a bit swamped by them. However, if you ask your friends, family and neighbours to give you a hand, they will come to your rescue. The most helpful person will be a young male, possibly the son of a neighbour who will be glad to help out, and even more so if there is a bit of pocket money in it for him. Why not ask your partner to help you too.

Saturday, 30th August
Moon square Mars

Many of the events taking place around you tend to put in a fairly depressive frame of mind at the moment. Sometimes it's too easy to see the universe as uncaring and harsh. What you need is an uplift in positive thinking. Too much negativity will take its toll on your health, so be kind to yourself and try to avoid disruptive events and people for today at least.

Sunday, 31st August
Sun conjunct Mercury

A good chat with a relative could open up possibilities and reveal old secrets today. The Sun meets up with Mercury in your solar house of heritage and family issues, so you'll take a great deal of pleasure in the company of those who are close to you. This should also be a time to look to the future. Perhaps moving home could be considered now.

September at a Glance

LOVE	♥				
WORK	★	★	★		
MONEY	$	$			
FITNESS	◍	◍			
LUCK	⋃	⋃	⋃	⋃	

Monday, 1st September
New Moon eclipse

Today's eclipse urges you to look far back into your childhood for the roots of the problems that now affect you. Many guilts, hang-ups and inhibitions remain from that time, and it's the perfect opportunity to rid yourself of these encumbrances. Recent events have forced you to question your place in a family or home that seems stifling and out of tune with your inner self. Today's events should help you make more sense out of the situation.

Tuesday, 2nd September
Venus opposite Saturn

You may feel like being carried away on a fluffy white cloud of romance, but harsh reality is likely to intrude. Reality may come in the form of some straight talking from a friend or two and, while you may not want to hear what they are telling you, in your heart of hearts you will have to admit that they are probably right. Children may turn out to be an obstacle to your dreams in some way now too.

Wednesday, 3rd September
Moon trine Neptune

Domestic bliss is on the cards today. The Moon unites with Neptune to provide a happy and harmonious atmosphere, both for you and all those within your family circle.

Thursday, 4th September
Moon trine Jupiter

There's a twinkle in your eye today, for the excellent aspect between the Moon and Jupiter enhances the romantic side of your nature. This is an adventurous influence favouring journeys in company with someone you love. If passion holds little appeal, then you should harness the good vibes to more creative projects because your talents shine now.

Friday, 5th September
Moon conjunct Venus

This should be a fun-packed day. The Moon and Venus get together in the most pleasurable area of your chart, surrounding you with friendly faces and a lot of laughs.

Female companionship is particularly stimulating and this will increase your self-confidence and belief in your talents. For the romantically inclined, attractions of a physical nature abound.

Saturday, 6th September
Sun sextile Mars

This is a great day on which to get any outstanding chores out of the way, especially those connected with your own personal property or premises. This means, for instance, your home, your garage or any kind of shop or business premises that you own or that you are closely involved with. You may have to do something to help your parents too, and the day will end with you feeling tired but pleased with yourself.

Sunday, 7th September
Mercury square Pluto

This will be an awkward day when other people let you down and leave you to sort out the wreckage. You are in the mood to talk, but your partner seems to be afflicted by temporary deafness and an inability to see things from your point of view. You should avoid signing anything binding today, possibly because you haven't looked at all the implications of what you are agreeing to.

Monday, 8th September
Moon sextile Neptune

If you've been prone to any stress-related complaints, you should see an improvement today. Pressure in your life seems to be easing now, and it won't do to take on too much just as things are getting better.

Tuesday, 9th September
Moon sextile Jupiter

This is a superb day for travelling. The influence of lucky Jupiter ensures a good time, especially if you are on the move in congenial company. Even if you make your journey alone, you'll be sure to find a companion along the way.

Wednesday, 10th September
Mercury direct

Mercury ends its retrograde passage across the sky today and turns once again to forward motion. The first area that you will notice being improved by this situation is that of your home and family. Items that you have mislaid will start to turn up now, and irritating things such as double-booking yourself so that you have to be in two places at once, will come to an end – until next time!

Thursday, 11th September
Venus square Neptune

The heart definitely rules the head today. In fact, it could be said that common sense has flown! You are likely to be swept away by the most unlikely passions and unrealistic dreams. When it comes to love or money, it won't be wise to commit yourself to anything today.

Friday, 12th September
Venus in Scorpio

Venus moves out of the fun, sun and pleasure area of your chart into the work, duty and health area, and it will stay there for the next few weeks. This suggests that any problems related to work and duty will become easier to handle, and also that you could start to see some kind of practical outcome from all that you have been doing lately.

If you have been off-colour recently, Venus will help you to feel better soon.

Saturday, 13th September
Moon conjunct Uranus

Faraway places and people should certainly influence your life today! You may be reassured by a letter or 'phone call from distant friends or family, or you could even fall in love with someone from a different culture or country.

Sunday, 14th September
Moon square Mars

Your new-found assertiveness in the workplace will inevitably earn you some enemies who think that you are getting above yourself. You know that this isn't the case and shouldn't worry about losing friends. True friends will understand what you are trying to achieve and applaud you for the effort you make. It's only the envious who will resent your rapid progress.

Monday, 15th September
Mercury sextile Venus

Your mind and your heart seem to be in harmony today. Your family are on your side and nobody wants to upset you. All is sweetness and light at work too.

Tuesday, 16th September
Full Moon eclipse

Eclipses have had a bad reputation since the time of the Romans, but eclipses have to occur on a particularly sensitive part of your chart for you to be affected personally. Today's little rotter will cause you some kind of unwelcome problem either at home, at work or both.

Wednesday, 17th September
Venus square Uranus

You seem to be very restless and probably in need of a holiday. It would be nice to just jump on a plane and take off for some sunny holiday destination now, but it seems highly unlikely that you can do so. Your women friends may give you unexpected problems today, or it may simply be that you are not in the mood to listen to their troubles. You may not be feeling all that well today either.

Thursday, 18th September
Moon conjunct Saturn

This is a good day for dealing with official or governmental people of any kind. You may have to 'phone your local tax office or your local council and it is possible that you may be asked to help with some kind of governmental or committee matter now. Older people will be particularly kind and helpful and, if you have older relatives to deal with, they will be in a pretty good mood too.

Friday, 19th September
Sun trine Neptune

It's quite a nostalgic time for you as the Sun makes contact with impressionable Neptune. You'll be happiest within your own surroundings reviewing happy memories. This sounds like a good day to get out the old photo albums.

Saturday, 20th September
Moon opposite Mars

Your mood is dreamy and distant today. You want to disconnect yourself from the world and all its demands and responsibilities. Unfortunately, an opposition between the Moon and Mars in the work sector of your chart today, will make this impossible to achieve. Keep your nose to the grindstone, your shoulder to the wheel and put your best foot forward. Later in the day, you can lay whatever is left of your body down for a nice rest.

Sunday, 21st September
Moon opposite Pluto

You will find it hard to work out what is going on in the minds of those nearest to you and, worse still, they will also find it very hard to understand your motives. This lack of mutual understanding may lead to a disagreement over money matters or something more important and much more subtle, such as when to begin a particular course of action or what road to take.

Monday, 22nd September
Sun into Libra

You are going to be in a slightly frivolous frame of mind over the next few weeks and you shouldn't punish yourself for this. Pay attention to a creative interest or a demanding hobby now or get involved in something creative on behalf of others. A couple of typical examples would be to be the production of a school play or making preparations for a flower and vegetable show.

Tuesday, 23rd September
Venus square Jupiter

Stress is causing some disruption to your routine at the moment. If you're prone to stomach upsets or heartburn, leave alcohol and spicy foods to another day. It's time to be good to your body, because if you are, your body will be good to you.

Wednesday, 24th September
Mars sextile Neptune

Tasks that you would usually shy away from become easy today. The energy of Mars will help you to get the most difficult or boring jobs out of the way quickly. You could be surrounded by workmen at some time during the day.

Thursday, 25th September
Moon opposite Neptune

It's not a good time to sign up for anything too complicated or legal. Hire-purchase agreements and loan arrangements should be left to another day. If you must sign on the dotted line today, then read all small print very carefully indeed.

Friday, 26th September
Sun sextile Pluto

The aspect between the Sun and Pluto could transform your personal life. Those who are married or otherwise linked will find your relationship entering a new phase. The single could find the love of your life.

Saturday, 27th September
Sun trine Uranus

Your emotions will be stirred up in an unusual manner today. You may fall head over heels in love with an unusually attractive person. Any such attraction will be sudden, electric and quite devastating. However, it may not stand the test of time. Instead of being whisked off to someone's boudoir, you could finish up in bed with a good book and a cup of cocoa!

Sunday, 28th September
Mars into Sagittarius

Today, Mars moves into the area of your chart that is devoted to relationships. This planetary situation is like a double-edged sword, because on the one hand it could bring you closer with your partner or loved one, while on the other hand you could feel extremely angry at the behaviour of others.

Monday, 29th September
Void Moon

This is one of those days when none of the planets is making any worthwhile kind of aspect to any other planet. Even the Moon's course is void, which means that it is not making any significant aspects. On such a day, avoid starting anything new and don't set out to do anything important. Do what needs to be done and take some time off for a rest.

Tuesday, 30th September
Mercury trine Neptune

This will be quite an easy day and there may be strange and subtle reasons for this. On the face of things, there may be no difference between today and many other days, but you seem to be learning the art of centring yourself and developing a kind of inner strength that helps you get through things more easily.

October at a Glance

LOVE	♥	♥	♥	♥	♥
WORK	★				
MONEY	$	$			
FITNESS	〰	〰	〰		
LUCK	☪	☪	☪		

Wednesday, 1st October
New Moon

There's a New Moon today casting a glow over your artistic potential. Your talents should shine now so believe in yourself and in what you can offer to the world at large. Of course, if art and literature leave you cold, you may be more inclined to an amorous path. Conventional values are not for you now since you're determined to be yourself and to chart your own course. Make time to have fun; you deserve it.

Thursday, 2nd October
Mercury into Libra

Mercury moves into a part of your horoscope that is concerned with creativity. Mercury rules such things as thinking, learning and communications, but it can also be associated with skills and craft work of various kinds. This combination suggests that the next few weeks would be a good time to work on hobbies such as dressmaking, carpentry and so on.

Friday, 3rd October
Mercury sextile Mars

You'll be a silver-tongued charmer today, with enough sex appeal to drive anyone wild with desire. You can use your seductive wiles to good advantage, because no one could possibly resist you.

Saturday, 4th October
Sun trine Jupiter

Anything that broadens your mind and gives new experiences is favoured by the Sun and Jupiter today. Travel is especially well starred, and this will also have a hint of romance. However, learning something for the pure joy of knowledge is also part and parcel of today's stars.

Sunday, 5th October
Mercury trine Uranus

Your intellect is on top form today. The speed of thought and the swiftness with which you grasp the most unfamiliar concepts will amaze those around you. A sudden urge to travel should be followed up.

Monday, 6th October
Venus sextile Neptune

Something strange seems to be working in your favour today because, although on the face of things, it looks as though everyone is against you, there seems to be an underground feeling that you are not altogether wrong and that you do have a point. If you have a close friend or a lover, take the opportunity to spend some time with them.

Tuesday, 7th October
Venus into Sagittarius

Venus, the planet of romance, moves into your horoscopic area of close relationships from today increasing your physical desires and bringing the light of love into your heart. If you're involved in a long-term partnership this is a chance to renew the magic of the early days of your union. If single, then the next few weeks should bring a stunning new attraction into your life.

Wednesday, 8th October
Jupiter direct

A lot of your convictions have gone through a profound alteration since Jupiter went retrograde. Today, the giant planet resumes its direct course and you can take stock of the changes you've experienced. A lot of confusions will now be resolved. You may feel that your luck improves as your mind clears.

Thursday, 9th October
Neptune direct

Neptune turns to direct motion today, and this will make it easier to cope with relationships of all kinds. You may have been so blinded by love that you haven't seen things as they really are, and you may have credited your lover with characteristics that he or she doesn't have. On the other hand, you may have been blaming someone falsely or laying all the faults of the world on someone else's shoulders. Neptune's direct motion from now on may help you to understand the truth of the matter a bit more clearly.

Friday, 10th October
Sun opposite Saturn

A socially awkward situation could get you and a loved one at loggerheads today. The main cause of this is pure embarrassment, either on your part or your lover's. Either way, it won't solve anything to make a scene.

Saturday, 11th October
Venus conjunct Pluto

There is no doubt about it, you are going through a really important time as far as personal relationships are concerned. This could be the time when you and your lover decide to turn what you have into a permanent arrangement. Even if you are alone and have no interest in getting together with anyone else, someone or something could change your mind today.

Sunday, 12th October
Venus sextile Uranus

Foreign affairs are likely to provide the highlights today. By that, we mean anything from an entertaining night out in an exotic restaurant to an affair with a foreigner! You can please yourself on a day when the most unlikely event will lead to a romantic interlude.

Monday, 13th October
Sun conjunct Mercury

Communication is the name of the game today as this will enhance all your relationships. You could have a really enjoyable chat to a friend or you could sit and talk things over with your lover today. You may decide to start a creative venture now and, if so, this is the time to research your ideas and see what materials and methods will best suit your purpose.

Tuesday, 14th October
Uranus direct

Uranus moves into direct motion today and this will bring a period of uncertainties and unpleasant surprises to an end. In your case this seems to be associated with overseas matters, so if you have friends or relatives overseas who have been experiencing difficulties, things should improve soon. Any problems associated with religion or the law will be resolved now.

Wednesday, 15th October
Mars sextile Jupiter

Happiness, optimism and adventure are the features of the day as Mars and Jupiter cast a marvellous aura over your chart. Seek out new experiences, get out and about with your partner and open your eyes to myriad of possibilities that await you. Unattached Geminis may possibly meet someone new.

Thursday, 16th October
Full Moon

Today's Full Moon could make you feel a bit tetchy and

tense, and it could also bring you some sort of unexpected expense. The best thing to do today is to stick to your usual routine and not start anything new or important. Jog along as usual and try not to become caught up in anybody else's bad mood now.

Friday, 17th October
Mercury square Neptune

There's a slightly seedy outlook today as your motives are not above question. You'll be prepared to use every trick in the book to get your own way, especially in affairs of the heart. You can be such a manipulator when you set your mind to it!

Saturday, 18th October
Venus sextile Jupiter

Getting to know someone else very well indeed will be particularly easy today. You'll be open-minded and receptive to ideas and emotional stimulation. Love could blossom while travelling or in an academic setting.

Sunday, 19th October
Mercury into Scorpio

The movement of Mercury into your solar sixth house of work, duties and health suggests that a slightly more serious phase is on the way. Over the next three weeks or so you will have to concentrate on what needs to be done rather than on having a good time. You may have a fair bit to do with neighbours, colleagues and relatives of around your own age soon, and you will have to spend a fair bit of time on the 'phone to them.

Monday, 20th October
Sun square Neptune

This is a bad time to make decisions about relationships.

Therefore, if you seem to have met the man or woman of your dreams, take some time out before making any promises, because you might be blinded by a rose-tinted infatuation just now. Much the same goes for money-making schemes or creative ideas. Just take everything a step at a time and it will be all right.

Tuesday, 21st October
Mars trine Saturn

A hope or ambition is likely to be fulfilled very soon. It won't exactly fall into your lap, since both Mars and Saturn encourage enterprise and effort on your part. However, if it's worth having, then it's worth putting yourself out for.

Wednesday, 22nd October
Mercury square Uranus

Your restlessness and boredom could have far-reaching consequences today. If your job is too tedious, you're likely just to walk out and do something far more interesting. If that's the case, we just hope that your job will still be there when you decide to return.

Thursday, 23rd October
Sun into Scorpio

The Sun moves into your solar sixth house of work and duty for the next month. This solar movement will also encourage you to concentrate on your health and well-being and also that of your family. If you are feeling off-colour, the Sun will help you to get back to full health once again. If you have jobs that need to be done, the next month or so will be a good time for action.

Friday, 24th October
Venus trine Saturn

Commitment, either to a person or to an ideal, is the main issue today. You'll be emotionally determined to give your time, efforts or even the remainder of your life to something or someone very important. For once, the heart dominates the head, but in this case it's no bad thing.

Saturday, 25th October
Venus conjunct Mars

Love, relationships and the good wishes of others are supremely important to you now. Oddly enough, you could be battling with a quite difficult opponent just now, but if you do have a powerful enemy around you now, the battle will be right out in the open rather than coming at you from some kind of hidden or unexpected quarter.

Sunday, 26th October
Moon sextile Mercury

Good news! If you are waiting for something to be fixed at home or at work, it will be. Frustrations will melt away as friends, neighbours and relatives rush round to help out with all those minor chores and problems that are plaguing you. An enjoyable neighbourhood event may provide some unexpected amusement, and pals who pop in may provide some more.

Monday, 27th October
Mercury square Jupiter

Just because you want a quiet time this Sunday, it isn't wise to fob others off with easy promises that you've got no intention of keeping. This isn't the way to keep friends or even any credibility. Of course you may think that your words will be fulfilled, but events out of your control decree otherwise. Keep your lips zipped.

Tuesday, 28th October
Sun square Uranus

Difficulties in the workplace could cause a sort of earthquake in the habitual running of your life. However, these disturbances could have a good effect in encouraging you to branch out into something that you really want to do, rather than sticking with a duty that you aren't too happy with.

Wednesday, 29th October
Moon opposite Saturn

You could be bored and irritable today and longing for something interesting to happen. Your usual sources of amusement don't seem to interest you now, and your friends and family are either unco-operative or busy with their own interests just now. Someone may annoy you by interfering with your usual routine or trying to 'supervise' your life or your work in some way.

Thursday, 30th October
Moon square Neptune

The unrealistic attitudes of a youngster will get on your nerves today. You won't be able to explain anything or even be understood. Try to be philosophical, and take the attitude that everyone has to make their own mistakes at some time.

Friday, 31st October
New Moon

Today's New Moon gives you the stamina to shrug off any minor ailments that have been troubling you. Occurring, as it does, in your solar house of health and work, it's obvious that you need to get yourself into shape to face the challenges that await you. A few early nights, a better diet and a readiness to give up bad habits such as smoking, will work wonders.

November at a Glance

LOVE	♥	♥	♥		
WORK	★	★			
MONEY	$	$	$	$	$
FITNESS	〽	〽	〽	〽	
LUCK	∪				

Saturday, 1st November
Moon conjunct Mercury

When the Moon makes contact with Mercury, mental powers are enhanced. You're very alert now especially when you have to deal with technicalities. If you're dealing with tradesmen, plumbers, domestic engineers and the like, you're very sharp. Unfortunately, since the solar house of health is also activated you may be prone to hypochondria today. More realistically, you may even suffer from some allergy or other. If in doubt consult your doctor.

Sunday, 2nd November
Moon sextile Uranus

Our suggestion may sound completely crazy, but you should try paying a visit to your in-laws today! If you can't visit them, then give them a ring to see how they are. The chances are that if you go to see them you will enjoy their company, and even if this is simply a duty visit you'll feel better for it. Your partner will spring a pleasant surprise on you later in the day.

Monday, 3rd November
Moon trine Saturn

A very practical plan will be presented by your partner or close friend. There may be a lot of work involved, yet this idea is splendid and deserves some serious attention.

Tuesday, 4th November
Sun square Jupiter

A disruption to your working day may turn out to be a blessing in disguise since it gets out of a familiar, if oppressive environment for at least a while. Take plenty of breaks today, because psychologically you need to see a few new faces.

Wednesday, 5th November
Venus into Capricorn

Today, Venus moves into your solar eighth house, signalling a couple of beginnings and endings in a rather vital part of your horoscope. You may decide to off-load a particular relationship now or to start a new one. This planetary aspect is not a terribly strong or important one, so it will not affect those of you who are in settled and regular relationships.

Thursday, 6th November
Moon conjunct Neptune

You'll be very sensitive to the moods and feelings of others today. On the one hand this is a good thing, bringing you and a partner into close emotional tune. However, you must be careful that you aren't persuaded into something that goes against your better nature.

Friday, 7th November
Mercury into Sagittarius

The inquisitive Mercury moves into your solar house of marriage and long-lasting relationships from today, ushering in a period when a renewed understanding can be reached between you and your partner. New relationships can be formed under this influence too, although these will tend to be on a light, fairly superficial level. Good humour and plenty of chat should be a feature for a few weeks, but you must try to curb a tendency to needlessly criticise another's foibles. Remember, not even you are perfect!

Saturday, 8th November
Moon square Mercury

You may find it hard to reach any kind of objective today. Your status and standing could be undermined in some way, possibly due to someone else putting in a bad word about you at your place of work. Colleagues could let you down and those whom you usually rely upon to get the job done efficiently could be unco-operative or even off sick just when you need them most.

Sunday, 9th November
Mars into Capricorn

Mars moves into your solar eighth house today, raising the level of your feelings to some kind of fever pitch. Your passions will be aroused in some important way and you could find yourself behaving in an unusual manner due to the depth of your emotions. Make sure that you are not simply reacting out of anger or due to some kind of feverish response.

Monday, 10th November
Mercury conjunct Pluto

You or your partner will have a bee in your bonnet and will get no peace until you have told somebody. If this attitude is a problem, then it's about time that it is discussed openly to clear the air.

Tuesday, 11th November
Mercury sextile Uranus

It's likely to be a day of good news. The influence of Mercury and Uranus brings glad tidings either from an official or legal source or from overseas. Sudden journeys or unexpected visitors will pleasantly take you by surprise.

Wednesday, 12th November
Moon square Neptune

Don't be too ready to lend cash or indeed to pick up the tab today. You could be easily taken advantage of by an unscrupulous acquaintance just now, so take care.

Thursday, 13th November
Moon trine Venus

Take the opportunity to show your loved ones how much you care today and, if you accompany your remarks with a gift of flowers or chocolates, so much the better. This will all be well received and much appreciated by your loved one. This may have a wonderfully reviving effect on your sex life. Well, it's worth a try, isn't it?

Friday, 14th November
Full Moon

Apart from a slightly frustrating Full Moon situation today, there is not much going on in the planetary firmament. The best thing to do is to stick to your usual way of doing things and to avoid starting anything new or important. If you feel off-colour or out of sorts, then try not to work too hard.

Saturday, 15th November
Jupiter sextile Saturn

A stroke of luck will enable you to make many of your hopes and wishes come true now. If you are involved in educational matters, the combination of Jupiter and Saturn favours your intellect. An older friend will be of great help to you.

Sunday, 16th November
Mercury trine Saturn

You and your partner should be in complete agreement now, and this is a day to communicate your hopes and desires. You'll find that they are in tune with those close to you. A serious talk will go a long way to solving apparent differences.

Monday, 17th November
Mercury sextile Jupiter

It just goes to show that you aren't all bad! It's fortunate that after some irritable outburst, there is someone who understands and still believes in you. It's obvious that you are an important pillar in someone else's life, so respond with some affection now.

Tuesday, 18th November
Uranus sextile Pluto

There's a revolution about to start concerning your close relationships. Don't panic, though, whatever occurs now is likely to be beneficial rather than otherwise. Perhaps old problems will now be resolved once and for all!

Wednesday, 19th November
Sun sextile Neptune

Things are changing, especially at work and in business relationships. Problems that seemed to be totally intractable are now beginning to melt away, and better times will surely come along soon. However, there is one little problem that you must be aware of, and that is your occasional habit of seeing things as you want them to be rather than as they are. So keep your eyes open.

Thursday, 20th November
Venus square Saturn

This is a very mixed day. The combination of Venus and Saturn shows that you'll have more than your fair share of unexpected hitches, complications and downright bloody-mindedness to cope with. You will be exasperated by the intransigent attitudes of others.

Friday, 21st November
Moon square Sun

It won't be a good idea to overload your schedule too much today. We know that you're bursting with self-confidence, but your vitality levels just aren't up to it at the moment. If you're working, the evening won't come around fast enough. If not, then leave domestic chores for now. A few unwashed dishes isn't the end of the world.

Saturday, 22nd November
Sun into Sagittarius

The Sun moves into the area of your chart devoted to relationships from today. If things have been difficult in a partnership, either personal or in business then this is your chance to put everything back in its proper place. It's obvious that the significant other in your life deserves respect and affection, and that's just what you're now prepared to give. Teamwork is the key to success over the next month.

Sunday, 23rd November
Moon trine Venus

This is not a day for duty. The lunar aspect to Venus puts a romantic spark in your soul, and there's nothing you'd like better than an intimate tête-à-tête with someone you love. Forget your worries for today at least and take that special person in your life out for a night of glamour. If you haven't got a special person, go for glamour anyway. Someone will catch your eye!

Monday, 24th November
Moon sextile Sun

Love is on your agenda today, so whether you are in the throes of a new love affair or whether you are happily settled in a relationship of long standing, all dealings with your other half will make you happy now.

Tuesday, 25th November
Moon square Mars

It'll be hard to keep anything in perspective at the moment since there's a harsh aspect between the Moon and Mars. Your feelings run high and you could experience a few emotional ups and downs. You're altogether too sensitive now and will rise to the bait in any conversation that could turn into an argument. If you want a quiet life, then keep your head down for a while.

Wednesday, 26th November
Mars square Saturn

Don't get involved in other people's disputes today. You may think that you are helping out, but you'll only end up getting the blame from both sides for sticking your nose in. Do yourself a favour and leave them to it!

Thursday, 27th November
Sun conjunct Pluto

You are in command today. In all dealings with others you'll be the one calling the shots and organising the routine. You won't be afraid of forcing change either, so more cautious folk had better watch out! This new mean, masterful you could be very attractive.

Friday, 28th November
Sun sextile Uranus

You could fall in love with an attractive and fascinating stranger today! Even if you don't actually go this far, you will certainly be attracted to someone new and you will probably be equally attractive to them in turn. Enjoy this flirtatious mood for what it is and be careful not to allow yourself to get into trouble – unless you want to, of course. You may be restless and in need of freedom today.

Saturday, 29th November
Moon conjunct Pluto

You are on the point of starting something quite new now, and although this could be almost anything, it seems to involve your home and family life. You may change your routine in some way, possibly because a family member has moved into or out of your home. You may have to make some kind of mental adjustment to what is going on around the house. There could be very good news about joint or family finances now.

Sunday, 30th November
New Moon

The only planetary activity today is a New Moon in your

opposite sign. It is possible that this could bring the start of a new relationship for the lonely but, to be honest, this planetary aspect is a bit too weak for such a big event. It is much more likely that you will improve on a current relationship rather than start a new one at this time.

December at-a Glance

LOVE	♥	♥	♥		
WORK	★	★	★	★	
MONEY	$	$	$	$	
FITNESS	Ⓜ	Ⓜ			
LUCK	℧	℧	℧		

Monday, 1st December
Moon conjunct Mercury

Today sees you at your subtle best. You're convinced that there's something going on, but you don't know exactly what it is. This puts you in your element. You'll be happily playing detective much of the time and you won't rest until you've uncovered the mystery. It goes without saying that your imagination is a trifle over-active, so be careful you don't put two and two together and end up with five!

Tuesday, 2nd December
Moon square Saturn

It could be easy to feel gloomy today since you'll assume that a friend has rejected you. Of course this isn't true, it's just that you pal has got a life too, and personal matters must take priority at the moment.

Wednesday, 3rd December
Moon conjunct Venus

The lunar conjunction with Venus in your house of habits and work shows that you want an extremely easy day. Anything that requires great effort has got to be put off, simply because you won't feel up to it. There are times when everyone needs to be pampered, and that's your mood now. It won't do you any harm to take a back seat for a short period and let everyone else get on with the business of living while you relax.

Thursday, 4th December
Sun trine Saturn

Common sense rules the day, but you are unlikely to be the one who comes up with any! Let other people do the planning today, and be content to follow their line of reasoning. Don't allow personal pride to interfere with practical reasoning.

Friday, 5th December
Moon conjunct Jupiter

This is really a day for optimism and happiness as the Moon contacts Jupiter. All your hopes are lifted by this harmonious combination. Of course you are now in a lucky period, but don't rely on it too much. You've got to put some effort into your life as well as fate.

Saturday, 6th December
Venus conjunct Neptune

You are very vulnerable today, which means that if some handsome guy or lovely lass decides to make eyes at you, you could find yourself falling head-over-heels in love!

If you are in a settled relationship, you will be gratified to discover just how much your lover wants you. You may be amazed by your own romantic and sexual response to any loving overtures made by others. Enjoy the day, as there aren't many like it!

Sunday, 7th December
Mercury retrograde

Life is always difficult when Mercury turns to retrograde motion, but the good news (if this is good news) is that everyone else will be affected in the same way as you. Over the next few weeks, messages will fail to arrive, business and money matters may become fouled up or delayed and, if you have to use a computer or any other kind of business machinery, it will be taken over by gremlins!

Monday, 8th December
Moon square Mercury

You may have to cancel an arrangement with a friend today, possibly due to having to run a few important errands for your partner or your working colleagues. If you need to go to the bank or the post office, allow plenty of time to get there or for waiting in the queue when you arrive. This is especially important if you have something more than the usual simple transaction to deal with.

Tuesday, 9th December
Sun sextile Jupiter

You may have felt very irritable lately, and perhaps prone to the odd temper tantrum. Luckily, your partner understands and still believes in you, so show them that their loyalty is appreciated.

Wednesday, 10th December
Moon trine Mercury

Rely on your instincts today, because they won't let you down. Sometimes the unconscious mind urges you in directions that the conscious ego wouldn't consider. Today you're at your intuitive best. You'll be able to detect the most subtle signals of the moods and true thoughts of those around you. This is an almost psychic influence that you'd do well to heed.

Thursday, 11th December
Moon square Jupiter

You're delving into your own private world again today. The power of your imagination is very strong and you can see things not as they are, but as they should be in an ideal world. You may review your life and realise how much you have learned as well as how much you've gained in the material sense.

Friday, 12th December
Venus into Aquarius

Today, the luscious planet Venus enters your ninth solar house. This will force you to spend the next month looking at ways in which you can expand your horizons. You may take a trip to somewhere new and exiting, or you could take up some kind of unusual or interesting educational opportunity. You may decide to delve into the art and mystery of cooking exotic dishes or growing unusual plants.

Saturday, 13th December
Mercury into Sagittarius

Mercury moves into the area of your chart that is concerned with relationships that are open and above-board now. This suggests that over the next few weeks you will have nothing to be secretive about in connection with your relationships with others. Your friendships will be free and easy and your lovers the kind whom you can happily take home to mother!

Sunday, 14th December
Full Moon

Today's Full Moon suggests that all is not well with at least one personal relationship. You may find someone close to you acting in a particularly awkward manner now, or you could find it absolutely impossible for you to get through to them.

Monday, 15th December
Mars conjunct Neptune

If you follow your intuition today, you won't go far wrong! Two areas are particularly sensitive now. In financial affairs you can pick up on subtle undercurrents and act on the information immediately to your eventual profit. In more personal affairs, intimate secrets and hidden passions will come to light.

Tuesday, 16th December
Saturn direct

The large, distant and rather gloomy planet, Saturn, turns to direct motion today and this will bring to an end a rather sticky and boring phase. You may have had to do without your usual friends and acquaintances over the past few weeks but they will soon be back to give you the help and support that you need. If you have been involved with difficult dealings with an official of some kind, this too will soon be solved.

Wednesday, 17th December
Sun conjunct Mercury

You and your lover have a great deal to talk over and today is the day to do it. If you are in the early stages of a relationship, you will find that you have a great deal in common and you will be content to while away many happy hours together discussing your childhoods and backgrounds. If you have something that is niggling you, don't keep this to yourself because it will linger, possibly causing long-term resentment.

Thursday, 18th December
Mars into Aquarius

You could find yourself travelling over great distances at some time over the next few weeks. You may be asked to visit friends or family who live overseas now, or you may simply take advantage of a good holiday offer. You may restrict your travelling to mental journeys by taking up a course of study or training now.

Friday, 19th December
Moon square Pluto

You will find it hard to cope with all the many and varied demands that are being placed on you at the moment. Your partner wants one thing, your family another and your job is also trying to claim a portion of your attention. You may feel like hiding away and forgetting the world for a while but you probably won't be able to get away with this. You could, if you are careful, manipulate things to suit you better.

Saturday, 20th December
Mercury sextile Jupiter

What an intellectually stimulating day this is likely to be! Your curiosity is on overdrive and you won't rest until you've found out everything you could possibly desire to know. Fortunately there are people around who will indulge your active mind.

Sunday, 21st December
Sun into Capricorn

Today, the Sun enters your solar eighth house of beginnings and endings. Thus, over the next month, you can expect something to wind its way to a conclusion, while something else starts to take its place. This doesn't seem to signify a major turning point or any really big event in your life but it does mark one of those small transitions that we all go through from time to time.

Monday, 22nd December
Venus conjunct Mars

Today's conjunction of Venus and Mars opens your eyes to numerous possibilities, both in the romantic sense and on a more cultural level. The aspect is undoubtedly good for all affairs of the heart, especially if you can share your insights with someone special. Art, music and theatre may also capture your interest.

Tuesday, 23rd December
Moon trine Jupiter

It's time to think ahead. Your personal life is in need of some attention as is your self-satisfaction in what you do. You need to display a creative and innovative side now; a holiday would be just the ticket. If you're attached then this could renew your relationship. If not, a meeting while away would fit the bill.

Wednesday, 24th December
Moon sextile Sun

The more normal and undemanding Christmas Eve the

better, as far as you're concerned. You won't want to stray too far from the straight and narrow, and you certainly won't want to immerse yourself in the madding (and maddening) throng!

Thursday, 25th December
Moon square Jupiter

You're likely to be bored by the jaded and familiar on this Christmas Day, and the normal run of things won't satisfy your taste for adventure at all. You need some innovation in your life, so steer away from the tried and true.

Friday, 26th December
Venus retrograde

You've probably had enough of domesticity for a while and would like to take a break from your familiar surroundings. On the other hand, your timing isn't that good, mainly because there are likely to be some cashflow problems to contend with before you can do a disappearing act and enjoy a break.

Saturday, 27th December
Mercury direct

Mercury gets back on the right course from today, and this should sort out some of the more difficult cash problems that have cropped up recently. Of course, not all will be solved overnight, so you'll still have to be a little careful with the finances for a while yet.

Sunday, 28th December
Moon conjunct Uranus

You seem to be on a strange wavelength now where you come across unusual people who introduce you to unusual and interesting ideas. You may be inspired or fascinated by something that you read or see on the television and, if it intrigues you enough, you may decide to look further into the subject. Friends may involve you in deep discussions about different religious or philosophical ideas.

Monday, 29th December
New Moon

Apart from a New Moon today, there are no major planetary happenings. This suggests that you avoid making major changes in your life just now but make a couple of fresh starts in very minor matters. You may feel like taking your partner to task over their irritating ways, but perhaps today is not the best day for doing this.

Tuesday, 30th December
Moon conjunct Neptune

You'll be deeply sensitive today and very susceptible to persuasion. Take care with all financial matters, because your judgement will not be at its best and you'll be easily swayed by persuasive talkers.

Wednesday, 31st December
Moon conjunct Venus

The year ends on a note of harmony and contentment. The Moon makes a splendid contact with Venus and this bestows the ability to enjoy life to its fullest. Any past family difficulties, such as rows with in-laws, can now be put behind you. You'll feel at one with the world.

ASTROLOGY FOR LOVERS

The Classic Guide to Love and Relationships

Liz Greene

This comprehensive guide to life, relationships and lovers provides an accessible and readable introduction to astrology.

Liz Greene, from her standpoint as trained psychotherapist and astrologer, explains the principles of astrology, debunks popular myths and shows how an understanding of the subject helps in forming lasting relationships.

Included are:

- the personality of each astrological sign
- an explanation of the shadow side
- the difference between the male and female of each sign
- how each sign behaves in love and out of love
- a quick guide to working out your ascendant sign.

UNDERSTANDING ASTROLOGY

A Practical Guide to the Stars

Sasha Fenton

Understanding Astrology provides a concise introduction to this ancient art, showing how it can be used to assess a person's character.

This book takes you beyond the person's 'sun sign' and shows you how to read birth charts. Every element of the horoscope is discussed in simple summaries, along with instructions on how to construct a chart for yourself.

Complete with sample birth charts and astrological tables, this book serves as an ideal starting point for anyone taking their first steps in the fascinating study of astrology.